THE SINNER'S CHARTER

Are the Ten Commandments for today?

Steve Maltz

Saffron Planet
PO Box 2215
Ilford IG1 9TR
UK
T: +44 (0) 7885 941848
E: contact@saffronplanet.net

ISBN 978-1-9163437-0-2

Cover design by Phil Maltz

Contents

Now why don't you …?

Introduction

It's a strange name for a book, perhaps even mischievous and misleading. I agree, but then when have I ever gone for safe titles? It's a book with a premise, an uncomfortable one, that considers those two tablets dragged down by Moses from Mount Sinai displaying words carved into the stone of such significance that God Himself read them out to a transfixed, but slightly trembling audience. This text is known by us as the Ten Commandments, an idea that has proved foundational to the processes that have driven Western civilisation ... until now!

Today, I suggest, the "Ten Commandments" have become a Sinner's Charter, a set of rules that may have started out as imperatives but, instead, now seem to have become skewed. It has all gone topsy-turvy, a flip in polarity of morality, governed not just by a relativistic atmosphere that brings us fake news and professional fibbing, but a 180 degree switchover, where right becomes wrong and wrong becomes ... well let's do it anyway because, frankly, does it really matter?!

Let's face it, the breaking of the "Ten Commandments" forms the basis of our entertainment industry, whether through movies, song or video games. You'd be hard pressed to find an "entertainment" where either, most or all of the "Ten Commandments" aren't spectacularly broken. Murder, adultery, robbery, blasphemy, dodgy worship (celebrity culture), lies and envy. They are all there in full splendour on a silver or flat screen or through speakers and headphones at your convenience. Just swipe your card to enter the world ... of possibilities. It is very telling that the only "entertainments" where this is not so (or to a lesser degree) are the offerings for our children (though that seems to be changing, looking at some of the latest Disney 'output'). We are keen to preserve their innocence yet, when we decide they are "adult" enough ... welcome to our sophisticated world where we feed ourselves on ever-more ingenious ways of breaking God's laws! Welcome to the Sinner's Charter.

Who is this book for? Although there is something for everyone within these pages, to both provoke and inspire, the journey that unfolds has been written for those who follow the Messiah, Jesus, the man who Moses spoke of (Deuteronomy 18:15), who would come to develop and deepen our understanding of God's laws, particularly these Ten Commandments. By doing so, he created a bridge between the "Old" and "New", forming one complete story of God's dealings with mankind, a story that is just as relevant today than it was to those Hebrews at the foot of Mount Sinai, where it all began ...

"The reason we have 17000 pages in our law books is because we cannot follow 10 lines on a tablet made of stone" Ravi Zacharias.

Prologue

Everything about this episode was unprecedented, never to be repeated, unique. A hinge of history was creaking into life as a bedraggled band of Hebrew slaves poured out of Egypt. It was so significant that it kick-started the Biblical calendar, with the month of Nisan and gave us the first of the three great Pilgrim festivals, *Passover*, that commemorated this Exodus from Egypt. These ex-slaves were true pilgrims, even if most were unaware of it. Some were even reluctant travellers, pining for the 'certainties' of the slave camps ('at least we got three square meals a day'). God was flexing His muscles in a big way, He was writing and directing a series of events that would, in the future, become His calling card, *"I am the God Who brought you out of Egypt ..."*

He first appears in a burning bush at the foot of a holy mountain, breaking into Moses' timeline and commissioning this reluctant octogenarian for the tasks to come, including multiple visits to the Egyptian ruler to warn him of dire consequences for thwarting God's plans. This Pharaoh had enslaved God's people out of fear that they may grow too large and become the enemy within. Instead they cried out to a half-remembered God Who, in turn, remembered them and brought ten plagues to Egypt, each announced in advance during Moses and his brother Aaron's multiple trips.

The plagues were direct challenges to the "gods" of Egypt. The first was the waters of the River Nile turning to blood, a blow to the supposed divinity of the river itself.

Then came frogs, a blow to the supposedly divine Pharaoh himself, who found these pesky critters even infesting his household! Then gnats, followed by flies. God was to show how He was the Lord of all, with infinite power, by limiting this latest plague to native Egyptian areas, ensuring that the Hebrew areas were bug-free. He did the same with the next plague on Egyptian livestock, with not a single animal death for the Hebrews. Again, this showed His supremacy over his rival "gods", who were powerless to act against Him. With the next plague, he also acted against Pharaoh's own magicians and astrologers, who couldn't even stand up through the boils that had infected their bodies, let alone try to reproduce the plagues themselves, as they did with the blood and frogs. That's the last we hear of them!

The next plague, hail, was a direct attack on Horus, the Egyptian sky "god". Before it, came a warning from God who told them *"by now I could have stretched out my hand and struck you and your people with a plague that would have wiped you off the earth. But I have raised you up for this very purpose, that I might show you my power and that my name might be proclaimed in all the earth."*(Exodus 9:15-16). There is a sense of an unfolding Divine drama playing out here with just a single underlying purpose … the Glory of God and His Name, the acknowledgment of He who brought His people out of Egypt. Then came hail, to show God's total dominion over the heavens as well as the Earth.

Locusts were next. God shows that He controls both the weather and animal life, bringing both together to destroy crops and that supposed Egyptian "gods" are incapable of stopping Him. This was followed by one of the dreads of mankind, complete darkness, again only in the Egyptian areas; the Hebrew areas must have seemed like a beacon mocking them in their powerlessness. Deprivation of social interactions through the darkness would have given them a sense of the awesomeness of Almighty God and again the inability of their 'home grown deities' to address the situation.

Finally, the killing of the firstborn, human and livestock. The Hebrews were saved by a simple action. God could have automatically exempted them, as He had done before, but this time He instructed them how to save themselves from the Angel of Death. They were to make a burnt offering of lambs without defect and then, *"they are to take some of the blood and put it on the sides and tops of the doorframes of the houses where they eat the lambs."* (Exodus 12:7). A physical act, often eulogised as the Hebrew households being saved from death through the blood of the lamb in the sign of the cross. Not totally accurate, but the sign was, in fact, of the Hebrew letter, *chet*, most often associated with the word, *chai*, meaning "life". Life was being offered to these households, all they had to do was to follow God's instructions. This is a beautiful picture, reminding us of our responsibility to respond to God's promptings, if we wish to enjoy *chai* in its fullest sense.

That night marked the beginning of their great adventure, arguably ours too, as over two million souls headed eastwards into the desert, including thousands of redeemed first-borns, saved by the faithfulness of their family. God has already shown His hand, His *outstretched* hand, but, over the next few weeks He is going to cement Himself to these people, a prelude to an important decision they were going to have to make regarding their future.

First, *guidance*. A pillar of cloud by day, a pillar of fire by night. A continual visual reminder of God's presence with them on their journey. And to make things as awkward as possible, He led them 'up the garden path' to the Sea, ensuring they were boxed in at the mercy of the advancing Egyptian chariots. They were to trust Moses and God, bringing *deliverance*, as the seas parted for them and subsequently destroyed their enemy.

And when the Israelites saw the mighty hand of the LORD displayed against the Egyptians, the people feared the LORD and put their trust in him and in Moses his servant. (Exodus 14:31).

Then, *provision*, whether it was clean water to drink, or manna and quail to eat, it was all supplied through miraculous means. How else were two million ex-slaves going to survive in a desert? He also showed them how a bunch of bricklayers were going to be able to defeat battle-hardened enemies. *Victory in battle* against the Amalekites! All Moses had to do was keep his arms raised, faith in God's promises was all that was needed. They knew that they were nowhere near strong enough to defeat this enemy, so God's strength was shown through their weakness.

A few weeks later Moses had gone full circle, he had arrived at the very holy mountain, Sinai, where he had been originally commissioned through the Voice at the bush. He had reached the end of the beginning and a new chapter for mankind was about to be opened ...

First the plagues, then release from Egyptian slavery, guidance, deliverance, provision, then victory over enemies. They were a people set apart, but what for? It wasn't long before they found out, as Moses summoned the elders and told them what God had said to him:

"This is what you are to say to the descendants of Jacob and what you are to tell the people of Israel: 'You

yourselves have seen what I did to Egypt, and how I carried you on eagles' wings and brought you to myself. Now if you obey me fully and keep my covenant, then out of all nations you will be my treasured possession. Although the whole earth is mine, you will be for me a kingdom of priests and a holy nation.' These are the words you are to speak to the Israelites." (Exodus 19:3-6).

The answer was a resounding YES, *we will do everything the LORD has said!* A nation was about to be born. They had to be prepared for what was to come, so, over the next two days the people washed their clothes and promised sexual abstinence, as barriers were created around the mountain, creating a no-go zone within for their own good for, whoever touches the mountain is to be put to death. Let's read what came next:

On the morning of the third day there was thunder and lightning, with a thick cloud over the mountain, and a very loud trumpet blast. Everyone in the camp trembled. Then Moses led the people out of the camp to meet with God, and they stood at the foot of the mountain. Mount Sinai was covered with smoke, because the LORD descended on it in fire. The smoke billowed up from it like smoke from a furnace, and the whole mountain trembled violently. As the sound of the trumpet grew louder and louder, Moses spoke and the voice of God answered him. (Exodus 19:16-19).

Let me repeat what I said at the beginning of this chapter. Everything about the following episode was unprecedented, never to be repeated, unique. A hinge of history was creaking into life. *Over two million people were about to hear the very Voice of God.* Unprecedented! It was said that, at that moment, not a bird chirped, nor a fowl flew, nor an ox lowed, not an angel ascended, not a seraph proclaimed 'holy'. The sea did not roll and no creature made a sound. All of the vast universe was silent and mute. And what were they about to hear? The foundational laws by which this new Nation – and subsequently all that followed – were going to live ... *the "Ten Commandments"*.

PART ONE
The Sinner's Charter

A declaration of authority

Actually, they are not *literally* the Ten Commandments. The Hebrew expression within the Scriptures is *Aseret ha-Dibrot,* which takes the meaning of the ten sayings, ten words or ten statements. The expression for Ten Commandments is very different, it would be *Aseret ha-Mitzvot,* in the same way that a *bar-Mitzvah* is a "son of the commandments". So why has the Church got it all wrong right from the outset? Not too sure, but perhaps "Ten Commandments" has a sense of immediacy and importance that the literal renditions lack? One thing is clear, though. By viewing them as a list of ten "commandments", the Church has missed out an extremely important chunk of Hebrew Scripture, *the preamble,* the first two verses in Exodus 20:

And God spoke all these words: "I am the LORD your God, who brought you out of Egypt, out of the land of slavery." (Exodus 20:1-2).

To Jews, this is the *first* commandment. In the vast majority of Christian Bibles, the actual commandments don't begin until verse 3, *"you shall have no other Gods before me."* By doing this the Church has missed two very important things; the fact that God was actually speaking these words and that He was declaring His calling card, His identifier, His USP (in marketing parlance) ... or, to take this further ... His supremacy, His uniqueness, His awesome power. The Church missed this, but the Jews didn't. If the Scriptures were a work of philosophy, God would be explained in some metaphysical sense, as taught by such as Aristotle. But they are not, they are a work of *revelation,* describing a God who has revealed Himself through His acts in history.

"I am the LORD your God."

Here is the same verse, in the ONE NEW MAN Bible, a modern translation that emphasises the Hebraic mindset behind the text.

"I AM the LORD your God."

Nowhere else would the capitalisation of two letters have such significance. This is a translation of the first Hebrew word in the verse, *anoki,* taking the meaning "I am". This very word is mainly used in the context of a royal command, a decree given for everyone. Its literal meaning is *Because I Am* and is used over a hundred times in Scripture.

You will notice the extra emphasis placed on those two words, **"I AM"** – capitalised in the One New Man Bible. It is God Himself speaking here and we're not to forget that. It underlines all that follows and puts a Divine seal on the proclamations that form the "Ten Commandments". These aren't ordinary instructions, these are coming from His very character, part of *God's eternal Word of life for all of us!*

Let's return to the foot of Mount Sinai …

The Hebrews did something that we canny consumers wouldn't dream of doing, they bought a set of goods *sight unseen!* Let's remind ourselves:

Then Moses went up to God, and the LORD called to him from the mountain and said, "This is what you are to say to the descendants of Jacob and what you are to tell the people of Israel: 'You yourselves have seen what I did

to Egypt, and how I carried you on eagles' wings and brought you to myself. Now if you obey me fully and keep my covenant, then out of all nations you will be my treasured possession. Although the whole earth is mine, you will be for me a kingdom of priests and a holy nation. These are the words you are to speak to the Israelites.' So Moses went back and summoned the elders of the people and set before them all the words the LORD had commanded him to speak. The people all responded together, "We will do everything the LORD has said." So Moses brought their answer back to the LORD. (Exodus 19:3-8).

Now read it again, *carefully.* God is selling them a concept, the idea of a covenant that they were to keep, but He *wasn't yet giving them the fine print.* They didn't yet know what was in the covenant, which rules they were going to have to obey in order to remain God's treasured possession. Later on Moses did read out the fine print, all 613 laws in the *Torah*, including the "Ten Commandments":

Then he took the Book of the Covenant and read it to the people. They responded, "We will do everything the LORD has said; we will obey." (Exodus 24:7).

The key word here is *obey.* There was no debate, no consideration of the minutiae, no deals or concessions over which laws should be prioritised, or which should be held back for further consideration! This was no 21st Century law court or debating chamber or political arena, these are a people listening and obeying, however strange many of the laws and regulations may have seemed to them at that time. There is a sense of this concept later on in the story, after Moses has read out the laws and summarised their importance to the Hebrews (and to all who were to come afterwards). There follows the most solemn and important prayer in Judaism, the *Shema*, Deuteronomy 6:4-5:

"Hear, O Israel: The LORD our God, the LORD is one. Love the LORD your God with all your heart and with all your soul and with all your strength."

The word *Shema* is the first word, usually translated as "hear". It is interesting that the majority of Bibles translate this word as "hear", but the One New Man Bible acknowledges that this word is far more powerful than it seems. It's not a case of just *hearing* but the actions that proceed from that process. It is about *obeying* God, in fact that is another meaning for *shema* elsewhere in Scripture. Hebraic understanding has no truck with just hearing but what effects the Word of God has on you. If you are not moved to action, then you haven't *really* heard.

These are a people who have pledged not just to listen or hear the words of the Law, including the "Ten Commandments", but to *obey* them. These words were going to become their manual for life. Let us now return to the prelude:

And God spoke all these words: "I am the LORD your God, who brought you out of Egypt, out of the land of slavery." (Exodus 20:1-2).

He is establishing and reminding us all of the authority that will undergird what follows. If these instructions were going to be obeyed in reality, then it had to be made clear Who was declaring them. It is all a matter of authority and this is a good place to consider the laws that we currently live under in 21st Century Britain. We will do so by looking at a case study, a controversial one, but one that will bring to light many pertinent points in our discussion.

On the 17th July 2013, the British Government passed the *Marriage (Same-Sex Couples) Act*. This now gives same-sex couples the opportunity to get married, just like any other couple. Subsequently, the first same-sex marriages took place in England and Wales on 29th March 2014, with Peter McGraith and David Cabreza from North London leading the pack. Here are the processes that brought about such an outcome.

Maria Miller was the Minister for Women and Equalities in David Cameron's Conservative government. She is happily married, with two sons and a daughter, so no axe to grind for her. Also, she had previously been non-committal over LGBT issues, yet, in May 2012, she urged Cameron to continue with proposals to introduce same-sex marriage in England and Wales and announced, in December that year, that same-sex marriage legislation would be introduced 'within the lifetime of this Parliament session'. In fact, the whole process only took a few months, with a First Reading of the Bill (proposal) in January 24th 2013, followed by a Second Reading two weeks later, which was passed by a large majority, of 400 to 175. The Bill was then examined by a committee, having received advice from the Church of England, the Catholics, the Church in Wales, two top QCs (one of whom was in my class at school!), various LGBT pressure groups, Liberal Judaism, the Board of Deputies of British Jews, Quakers, Unitarians, Methodists, the United Reform Church, a few prominent individuals and the *Coalition for Marriage*, a Christian anti-'same sex marriage' group. No amendments were made and the process continued.

The Bill was then examined by a group within the House of Commons and a few amendments were made. It then received its Third Reading on 21st May and passed with a majority of 366 to 161. It was then passed over to the House of Lords on the same day with a First Reading, followed by a Second Reading on 4th June, when an attempt was made to scupper it by Lord Dear, which failed miserably. The Bill was passed to a House of Lords committee later in June and a few more amendments made, then it passed to the Report Stage, where a few more tweaks were implemented. On 15th July it had its Third Reading, where it passed simply by a voice vote, a cascade of 'ayes'. The final Bill was approved the next day by the House of Commons and the Queen gave her Royal Assent the day after. It was now enshrined in the Law of the Land. The whole process took six months, *about half the time an average Bill would take,* from First Reading to Royal Assent.

So that's how we do things these days. There is a perceived need to address a situation, usually motivated by "progressive" thinking, of moving society forwards on a path dictated by such concepts as 'equality' or 'inclusion'. Although a wide consensus is sought, as we saw from the experts consulted on the same-sex marriage issue, there seems to be a gathering momentum to push certain issues through. Yet, at the end of the day, we have laws passed from the mind of man. *Does God get a look in?* Was He consulted on this issue? Certainly, there was a strong "religious" input, not just from the Church (in various forms), but from Jewish concerns as well and concessions were made in the form of amendments for Churches to "opt-out" according to their convictions. Yet the Bill itself passed despite the efforts of a dwindling Christian presence among our "ruling classes", although nine Anglican bishops (including Justin Welby) joined Lord Dear in trying to scupper the Bill (five other bishops abstained). At the time of writing, Northern Ireland is holding out. Their Assembly has voted on it five times to date and each time the *Same-sex marriage Bill* has been vetoed by the Democratic Unionist Party, staunch and uncompromising Christians. They are also the only political party who unanimously opposed the Bill in its various Readings in the House of Commons!

We have come a long way from the "Ten Commandments" and the rest of the *Torah*.

And God spoke all these words: "I am the LORD your God, who brought you out of Egypt, out of the land of slavery." (Exodus 20:1-2).

A Law that has been initiated in the Mind of God is going to be a good one, undergirded by absolute truth and unsullied by the agendas of man. It can be trusted, even if it is not completely understood as in the case of some of the stranger statutes and regulations among the 613 given in Genesis to Deuteronomy, the five Books of Moses, the *Torah*.

A Law that has passed through Parliament onto our statute books, has passed through the mind of man and the various agendas of influential groups in our current society. It will be tainted by compromise and bartering between the relative truths of all the people who will be affected by the Law. It will be a Law that works according to the current climate and, if it doesn't work so well as society changes, then it will go through further amendments and compromises. It is a fluid situation, *there's no more carving on tablets of stone for our lawgivers!*

This is, after all, how the world works these days, or rather the kingdom of the World. The "Ten Commandments" came from a very different mindset, the kingdom of God. We need to understand the dynamic that exists between them. Although God is ultimately in control of all earthly powers ...

Let everyone be subject to the governing authorities, for there is no authority except that which God has established. The authorities that exist have been established by God. (Romans 13:1).

... Satan has been currently given control of the Kingdom of the World.

"I will not say much more to you, for the prince of this world is coming. He has no hold over me." (John 14:30).

We have a foot in both camps, we live in the World's kingdom but we are governed by the principles of God's Kingdom, guided and empowered by God's Spirit. When we provide a good witness of God, then we are demonstrating a flavour of God's Kingdom to those living by a very different set of rules. In the matter of the *same-sex Marriage Bill* those Northern Irish politicians did that very thing and, by doing so, stood up for the truth and the principles that guide them as people of God.

I chose this example of a man-made Law because it is very relevant to those foundational verses I have been so fond of repeating:

And God spoke all these words: "I am the LORD your God, who brought you out of Egypt, out of the land of slavery." (Exodus 20:1-2).

God has chosen to deal with mankind through covenants, some made with individuals, such as Abraham, Moses and David, but others as general agreements to cement our relationship with Him. One such covenant regards marriage.

"For this reason a man will leave his father and mother and be united to his wife, and the two will become one flesh." This is a profound mystery—but I am talking

about Christ and the church. However, each one of you also must love his wife as he loves himself, and the wife must respect her husband." (Ephesians 5:31-33).

Here Paul tells us that something as sacred as Christ's relationship with the Church is a mystery modelled in the flesh by man's relationship with his wife within the marriage bond. If we meddle with the model, then we are mocking something sacred and dear to the Heart of God. To redefine marriage is to taint the Holy covenant that is at its heart. When God declares out loud that it is He who demonstrated His mighty powers to the Hebrews and that our side of the bargain is to keep the laws He has made for us for our own good, He is also declaring us as a people bound to Him by covenant. *He reminds us exactly Who we are dealing with,* even those of us reading these words thousands of years later and we meddle with His Words at our peril, particularly those of us in covenant with Him.

If the Kingdom of the World seeks to redefine marriage, it is their business because all they are doing is borrowing a technical term and tweaking it according to their own agenda. But on no account should they expect to have God's seal of approval on what they are doing. The danger is when Christians are sucked into this, allowing the Kingdom of God to be tainted. Beware, Church, you really don't understand Who you are dealing with. *They sow the wind and reap the whirlwind.* (Hosea 8:7).

One last time:

And God spoke all these words: "I am the LORD your God, who brought you out of Egypt, out of the land of slavery." (Exodus 20:1-2).

In the Jewish Haggadah (the guidebook for Passover Seder services) it declares that in each generation each person is obligated to see themselves as if they personally came forth from Egypt. That should be equally valid to those of you "grafted in" to the Jewish (Abrahamic) covenant. We should be owning these words.

It's a declaration of His authority. It is laying the ground for those words that follow, etched on stone tablets and etched on the hearts of all who call themselves people of God. *The Sinner's Charter* would seek to ignore this declaration, (as, sadly, do many in the Church too). Or, instead, it is substituting it with the following words:

And Parliament brought forth Laws. "Our authority is as elected politicians, who you must trust to guide you through our wisdom and desire for only the best outcomes."

The story begins …

Who are the 'powerful ones'?

2

"You shall have no other gods before me." (Exodus 20:3).

The literal reading of this verse in the original Hebrew is:

"Another powerful one will not exist for you in My Presence."

This is, of course, an acknowledgement that there are other 'powerful ones' or 'gods' out there that could lead the Hebrews and, by extension, us too, astray. It is interesting that famed Jewish sage, *Rashi*, translates the term as "gods of others", which is perfectly feasible bearing in mind that Biblical Hebrew is not the easiest to translate, in that only consonants are in the original script, the vowels were added later. This gives us leeway in translating into English and also, as a consequence, puts us at the mercy of the translators and their mindsets. Rashi's translation makes an important point. If we use the expression "other gods" then we are acknowledging the existence of rivals to the One True God, but if we use "gods of others" or "gods of other nations" we are distancing these rivals and minimizing their power to sway God's people.

In our current multicultural society "gods of other nations" are not *over there* any more but are very much *over here*. In a legal sense, it all began in 1858, when, after the *Indian Rebellion*, Queen Victoria told Indians that they are now British subjects and would enjoy religious toleration. They were *Hindus*, though the concept itself was a British invention, referring to rulers in India who were neither Muslim nor Christian! Ordinary Indians at the time preferred to define themselves according to matters of family, caste, region of origin and sectarian inclinations, with huge varieties in terms of rituals and "gods" to worship. The British were fascinated by this 'rich tapestry' and enormous collection of 'gods', currently running at around 33 million, including the elephant-headed *Ganesh*, *Shiva* the destroyer and the wrathful *Kali!*

The person most responsible for *anglifying* Hinduism was Swami Vivekananda, who tirelessly popularized the religion in lecture halls throughout England and the USA. He sold Hinduism as the most ancient source of spirituality, merging it with western materialism and making it more palatable for potential converts. Another major factor was the activity of a mystical cult known as the *Theosophical Society,* formed in 1875 by Helena Blavatsky, which merged Hinduism with occultism and the Kaballah with a stated objective of bringing religions together and making sense of the universe. Since then there have been four waves of Hindu immigration to England; after the Second World War in 1947, in the 1960s to help save the NHS, which was running out of doctors, in the 1970s expulsion from Uganda by Idi Amin and in the 1990s, as refugees or for economic advancements. Hinduism is currently the third largest religion in England, representing over 1.5% of the population.

Islam has been influential indirectly, through its philosophical ideas and scientific advancements since the Middle Ages. Some early Protestants were quite favourable to the religion and there were alliances made with the Turkish Ottoman empire in the 16th Century. In the 17th Century, academia fell in love with Arab culture and Arabic was taught at Oxford and Cambridge universities. Arabic literature, such as the *Arabian Nights*, was translated into English. In terms of the Muslim population, the first to arrive in any quantity were sailors from India in the early 18th Century one of whom, Sake Dean Mahomet, opened the first Indian restaurant, the *Hindoostane Coffee House*, in 1810.

One by-product of the success of the British Empire, was the huge number of 'subjects' pulled in. By 1911 there were far more Muslims than Christians in the Empire, growing to around half the world's Muslim population by the 1920s! Mass immigration to England started after the Second World War, to help rebuild the country, including, as with the Hindus, a huge influx of Muslim doctors to shore up the NHS in the 1960s, encouraged by the health minister ... Enoch Powell. Currently Muslims account for around 5% of the population, the second biggest religion in England and Wales.

Buddhism hasn't been around on these shores quite as long as the other two. It probably all kicked off in 1924, with the foundation of *London's Buddhist Society*. It was seen as a contemplative, monastic tradition and there was a lot of to-ing and fro-ing to Asian retreats to top up the spirit levels. Around 0.5% of the English population are Buddhists, around the same as the Jewish population.

So 'the gods of other nations' have very much made their home in Britain. It used to be that the responsibility for integration into 'British ways' was firmly at the feet of these immigrants, but times have now changed with the advent of *multiculturalism* as one of the strongest forces in society. It is the indigenous population (nominally Christian) that is now expected to adapt and change and 'British ways' are painted with very broad strokes. On the face of it this would seem to be a positive step, particularly for those of us who have a 'progressive' outlook on life, but we must balance the advantages with the costs involved.

Before we start getting all 'political' and retreat into our chosen positions for the battles to come let's remind ourselves of what Kingdom we inhabit and Who is the Master of our lives. We often default to human perspectives, even those of us who are Christians and fail to ask the most important question of all ... *what does God think of this?*

First the human perspective. Some quotes on multiculturalism:

"We become not a melting pot but a beautiful mosaic. Different people, different beliefs, different yearnings, different hopes, different dreams." Jimmy Carter.

"Pit race against race, religion against religion, prejudice against prejudice. Divide and conquer! We must not let that happen here." Eleanor Roosevelt.

"The deal with multiculturalism is that the only culture you're allowed to disapprove of is your own." Martin Amis.

That last quote is quite telling because it is true to say that the current focus is on how flexible Christianity is in order to live comfortably with rival worldviews, specifically 'gods of other nations'.

It is tempting and wrong to draw parallels with the ancient Hebrews in their relationship with the 'gods of other nations' that had insinuated themselves into their society. Penalties were severe and were laid out quite clearly in the *Torah*.

"Whoever sacrifices to any god other than the LORD must be destroyed." (Exodus 22:20).

Of course, the seduction of God's people by these 'gods'

was to lead to permanent exile in Assyria and temporary exile in Babylon, so it was clear that punishment was not going to evade these errant people. OK, those were different times, but what of today? How do we live with our Hindu, Muslim and Buddhist neighbours? *What does God think of the 'gods of other nations' that live with us?*

We must never forget that the Israelites, on accepting God's offer at Sinai, were now His special people, a holy incubator for God's promises. They were to be His witnesses to the Nations, His possession. It was no trivial undertaking; they were His public face to the World. God was feared and respected when they won battles in His Name, but not so much when their conduct fell below the high standards expected for a people cemented together by a set of Laws governing all aspects of their life. But most importantly, they were to provide the means to produce the Messiah for all mankind. The messianic line had to be protected at all costs, despite all the enemy would throw at it to destroy it before it brought forth that helpless baby in the Bethlehem stable. For this reason, God had to be strict with His people, even if it meant some pruning. There was a Divine purpose, one not given to any other people at any time in human history.

There is a parallel situation in today's society. Christians live alongside followers of other gods and no gods. Some of us will fall by the wayside, as did a good proportion of those ancient Jews. But for the rest, there is a purpose. It is called the *Great Commission*.

"Therefore go and make disciples of all nations, baptizing them in the name of the Father and of the Son and of the Holy Spirit, and teaching them to obey everything I have commanded you. And surely I am with you always, to the very end of the age." (Matthew 28:19-20).

We must consider the possibility (or probability) that fulfilling this purpose does not necessarily entail travel to far-flung corners of the world to 'evangelise the heathens', as it was in earlier centuries. The mission field is now on our doorstep, often literally. Those who follow other faiths are not our enemies, the nations are now among us. We are called to make disciples of them, show them the truth of the Gospel. And unlike those ancient Jews, we not only have the incentive to do this, but God has equipped us with His Word and His Spirit to help us in this life-transforming task. There seems to be a major contrast between now and then; the danger with the ancient Israelites was the seductive appeal of the 'gods of other nations', but perhaps this appeal is not so strong these days. Rather than fearing losing folk to other religions we should, instead, get our act together and concentrate on making disciples of the nations among us.

Wrenching people away from 'other gods' is not an easy task though, and it is certainly not the 'politically correct' thing to do in our multicultural society, where we are called to respect and tolerate other faiths and let others live in peace. The Kingdom of the World says STOP but the Kingdom of God says GO … and make disciples. It's what God has put us on Earth for.

We must never forget that 'the gods of other nations' are still rivals to the One True God and man certainly can't serve two masters, whether it is the *Allah* of the Muslims or the millions of Hindu varieties. We remind ourselves:

"You shall have no other gods before me." (Exodus 20:3*)*.

Multiculturalism gives each equal billing, it accepts no place of favour for the Christian God, despite the fact that Britain has been a Christian nation (of sorts) since Roman times. Each religion is deemed free to exist within its own bubble, with its own set of truths and woe betide anyone who attempts to disrupt this artificial sinister construct. In reality, Christianity is deemed *least among equals*, thanks to the machinations of cultural Marxism (explained thoroughly in my book, *Into the Lion's Den*), condemned by the misguided actions of some in the past who used a Christian smokescreen to mask actions that were no way condoned by the Bible, such as slavery, persecution and misogyny. Religious "freedom" comes as part of the package, as long as it is not the Christian religion being defended. For instance, *Islamophobia* is a word bandied about a lot, particularly when there is a fear of reprisals after the latest terrorist outrage by Islamists. Yet the word implies an irrational fear, that's how a phobia is defined, and there is nothing irrational about the negative emotions stoked up by actions inspired by the writings of Islam. Yet there is no such thing as *Christophobia*. Isn't that curious? Of course this is not to condemn Muslims any more than to condemn the vast majority of Christians in history who had absolutely nothing to do with the hateful things done 'in the name of Christ', such as the Inquisition, anti-Semitism and the Crusades.

Our culture now feels uncomfortable with the name "Christmas", renaming seasonal events in order not to give offense to followers of other faiths, despite the fact that, mostly, Muslims and Hindus are unconcerned and frankly puzzled why this should be happening. Perhaps it's the jarring reference to *Christ* in the name, which perhaps explains why Easter is not targeted, as it has been redefined as a season of bunny rabbits and chocolate eggs and therefore satisfactorily neutralized!

In October 2013 there was a motion in Parliament to end swearing on the Bible when giving oaths in court,

"I swear by Almighty God to tell the truth, the whole truth, nothing but the truth." Instead witnesses would be just asked to sincerely promise to tell the truth. Of course, many who take a Biblical oath are no longer motivated by a fear of Divine retribution if caught lying, yet there is power in the symbolism and a significant shift in power if the symbol is removed. Unsurprisingly, multiculturalism has allowed the *Qu'ran* and other holy books to be used for followers of other religions. Atheists just need a sincere affirmation. The motion was defeated, though it didn't stop the Boy Scouts and Girl Guides from moving God out of their oaths.

Christianity has a distinctive from all other religions. It is by its core nature *evangelistic*. It is a grafted-in faith, not an inherited one. You are not born a Christian, it is a personal decision made in collaboration with the Holy Spirit and a direct result of the Great Commission. You are brought into the Family of God through the actions of the Holy Spirit and as a result of the words, deeds and prayers of others, except in cases where God acts sovereignly, as is His prerogative.

Although Islam does have evangelistic elements, judging by the increasing number of converts, promoting the faith is not considered one of its *five pillars*, these being faith, prayer, charity, fasting and pilgrimage. Converting to Islam is mostly due to the shortcomings of the alternatives, whether the liberalism, perceived prejudice or lack of direction in the Church or the moral corruption of our secular society. Those who convert to Buddhism tend to be those on personal spiritual journeys, something encouraged by Buddhist teachings and, again, tends to be a reaction to the materialism, control and pointlessness of our capitalist society. It's a similar situation with Hinduism, a desire for eastern mysticism over western materialism, something of great interest to those wealthy western materialistic pop stars, such as the Beatles, who dabbled with Hinduism in the 1960s but ultimately mostly felt drawn back to the material comforts of Rolls Royces, mansions and sumptuous living.

So multiculturalism presents us with a menu of "gods" and I haven't even got started on Sikhism, Taoism, the Bahais, as well as the endless varieties of "Christian" cults, such as Mormonism and the Jehovah Witnesses. Rather than acknowledging the reality of the One True God (with the disclaimer that ... and of course there are other "gods" you may want to consider ...), it relegates *Our Father in Heaven, the Creator of the Earth and the Heavens* to an equal standing with the *Great One-eyed Tothz the Magnificent.* We remind ourselves:

"You shall have no other gods before me." (Exodus 20:3).

This is not a suggestion, it's a warning, and where warnings are unheeded, there are always consequences. Consequences for the ancient Israelites were exile, exclusion; even death. Consequences today are, perhaps, even more troubling, *the danger to one's own eternal soul.* Evangelism has never been more challenging ... or important.

In the Sinner's Charter, our modern day 'version' of the Ten Commandments, the first commandment has been redefined and incorporates an overt rejection of the One True God, or at the very least offers Him as an alternative to all the other "goods" ("gods"?) on display. Here is a suggestion:

"You can have any gods you like, as long as you don't encourage others to believe as you do."

Worship on the sly

"You shall not make for yourself an image in the form of anything in heaven above or on the earth beneath or in the waters below. You shall not bow down to them or worship them; for I, the LORD your God, am a jealous God, punishing the children for the sin of the parents to the third and fourth generation of those who hate me, but showing love to a thousand generations of those who love me and keep my commandments." (Exodus 20:4-6).

There are four connected narratives here. Here's the first:

"You shall not make for yourself an image in the form of anything in heaven above or on the earth beneath or in the waters below."

The Hebrew word translated as "image" is *pecel* and although the context implies something carved or sculpted, it can refer to any three-dimensional image, however it is produced. Suddenly we can see the relevance to today, in our image-conscious society. Stone and clay give way to pixels, whether graphics or videos displayed on a smartphone or huge experiences in 3D cinemas or huge glittering electronic billboards. Images are everywhere, imploring us to buy, to experience … dare I say *to worship?* But perhaps we are jumping ahead of ourselves, as the clear message here is the prohibition against the making of the image, rather than what it is used for. Is this a specific condemnation against graphic designers, animators, artists, even if their talents are not knowingly being used in ungodly ways? As ever, the clue is in the context.

The prohibitions concern images of anything in heaven above or on the earth beneath or in the waters below. Is this significant? Yes, it was to the immediate audience for these words. In those days, *things in the heaven*, such as the sun, the moon and the stars, were certainly worshipped by the pagan nations. So anyone who created such an image can be held responsible. *Things on the earth beneath* alluded to natural features such as rivers, trees, hills and mountains, that were deified and therefore abhorrent to God. This could also include statues made to commemorate mere mortal beings such as Pharaoh and Nebuchadnezzar, who considered themselves "gods". Again, the very objects themselves were an affront. *Things in the waters below* was a reference to demons, who would conceal themselves down below and, as archaeology has shown us, were well catered for in the form of idolatrous images of stone and clay.

Tearing ourselves away from the past, the prohibitions for today would be for anyone guilty of creating images for the overt purpose of worship, such as porcelain Buddhas, icons of the Virgin Mary and such objects that may be found in ecclesiastical gift shops.

"You shall not bow down to them or worship them" ...

This is where it gets serious as we are soon going to read about consequences. It's one thing to be creating such abhorrent objects, but it's a far more serious matter when we are prostrating ourselves before these objects. And because we are living in very different days to the Ancient Israelites, everything broadens out as we consider modern equivalents to those images of stone and clay and look behind the form, at the *function*. In short, God is unhappy *at anything that we bow down to and worship.* And this can take many forms in our modern society:

- Prominent people who you respect / feel attracted to / empower you / entertain you. These are products of the media of the day. In the 19th Century it would be the explorers, scientists or writers who would be featured in the daily rags and penny pamphlets, in the early days of the cinema it would have been film stars, in the TV age it would have broadened to pop stars and 'celebrities' in general and in our internet age it can be absolutely anyone, irrespective of any talent or redeeming features.

- Anything actually produced by one of the above groups, such as pieces of music, films, art etc. I know someone who has seen the *Sound of Music* fifty-eight times – is that the best use of their time? Obsessional behaviour is self-destructive and certainly gives no glory to God and instead mars His image that lives within us.

- Anything in God's Creation that may cause you to worship the Creation rather than the Creator. The correct behavior is that the beauty of the Creation should bring us to our knees to praise and thank God Himself.

They exchanged the truth about God for a lie, and worshiped and served created things rather than the Creator--who is forever praised. Amen. (Romans 1:25).

Now of course we are not physically bowing down and worshipping the above (though I'd make an exception at some behavior I've seen at football games) but it's not the externalities we need to concern ourselves with but the inner motivations and impulses. We human beings were made to worship, it's a natural God-given impulse within each of us, yet when the object of our worship isn't God Himself then something has got very skewed along the way.

A philosopher once asked Rabbi Gamaliel the Elder (the same one as in Acts 22:3), *"if idols of other gods are so dead and powerless, yet they still led the Israelites away from God, then why didn't God just destroy them all?"* The Rabbi replied, *"Do they worship just idols? They also worship the sun, the moon, the stars and the constellations, the mountains, hills, springs and valleys, even their fellow men! Should God destroy His whole creation because of these fools?"*

A good reply and a pointer to our restless souls that just need to worship something and that, if we are so blind as to ignore our Creator, then we are liable to shower our affections and loyalty on a whole number of worthless substitutes.

There's also a subtle and insidious form of false worship that involves the energy we expend in our search for money and success. *Mammon*, that persistent false idol! Job claimed to be untouched by this in his self-justification:

"If I have put my trust in gold or said to pure gold, 'You are my security,' if I have rejoiced over my great wealth, the fortune my hands had gained, ..." (Job 31:24-25).

We read of Abraham accumulating much cattle and was, in his day, quite a wealthy man. But money was not an end in itself, it wasn't an idol to worship and we trust that he used his wealth responsibly.

"For I, the LORD your God, am a jealous God, punishing the children for the sin of the parents to the third and fourth generation of those who hate me" ...

And here are the consequences of misplaced worship.

The only place in Scripture where God is termed 'jealous' is here, when dealing with idol worship. When the Israelites accepted God's offer at Sinai to be His favoured nation, His Kingdom of priests, what we saw in effect was a marriage, a bond of matrimony created between God and His 'chosen people'. A Jew worshipping 'another god' is as a spouse engaging in adultery so God, the jilted partner, has every right to respond in jealous anger. The Hebrew word used here for 'jealous', *qanna*, is related to a similar word, pronounced the same but featuring an 'h' (*hey*) rather than a silent "a" (*aleph*) as its final letter. This word takes the meaning of 'owning', giving the sense that the Israelite nation was God's possession and no foreign "god" has the right to entice His people away from Him. So the bond between the Creator and His chosen people was a strong one, explaining why punishments for breaking this bond were going to be severe.

Yet the punishment seems unfair. Why should the kids, grandkids and great-grandkids suffer for our mistakes? Before we judge according to our own standards – which is a dangerous thing to do of course and quite inadvisable – let's see if the Bible provides us with examples of this principle actually working.

The one that really comes to mind is the result of the lengthy reign of wicked old King Manasseh. I wrote about this in *God's Blueprint*: You can't choose your family and Hezekiah's son, Manasseh, was probably the worst King of all. *"And he did that which was bad in the sight of the LORD, after the abominations of the nations, whom the LORD cast out before the children of Israel."* (2 Kings 21:2).

Manasseh was the straw that broke the camel's back and it is because of his many evil acts that God chose to hold back no longer:

And the LORD spoke by His servants the prophets saying, "Because Manasseh king of Judah has done these abominations, having done wickedly above all that the Amorite did, who were before him, and has made Judah also to sin with his idols: therefore thus says the LORD God of Israel, Behold, I am bringing such evil upon Jerusalem and Judah, that whoever hears of it, both his ears will tingle." (2 Kings 21:10-12).

But this doesn't happen during his reign. Ironically it happens during the reign of his saintly grandson, Josiah, the righteous King who discovers the ancient scrolls of the *Torah* and dedicates his people to God, cleansing the land and the people:

And there was no king before him like him, who turned to the LORD with all his heart, and with his entire being, and with all his might, according to all the Torah (Teaching) of Moses, nor did any like him rise after him. (2 Kings 23:25).

But, in the very next verse:

Nevertheless the LORD did not turn from the fierceness of His great wrath, by which His anger was kindled against Judah because of all the provocations with which Manasseh had provoked Him. (2 Kings 23:26).

God brought judgement in the reign of Josiah's son, *the fourth generation since Manasseh.*

One could see this principle as an effective deterrent to a people who cherished family relationships above everything. The period spanned by four generations is probably the upper limit for them all to be alive together and so, for someone's sins to have an effect on one's great-grandchildren would provoke feelings of sheer shame and horror. In modern history one wonders how our unforgiving culture would deal with any near descendants of such as Stalin, Hitler and their demonic henchmen.

Then, finally, there's a more positive spin offered:

... but showing love to a thousand generations of those who love me and keep my commandments.

Here's a concrete statement of God's mercy trumping judgement. If you misbehave then your shame is going to be paraded to your living descendants, but if you behave yourself then your legacy will shine throughout all future days. Some translations prefer the term 'thousands of generations', which is close enough to saying 'forever' as you can get. If this is not an incentive for leading a good and faithful life, then I don't know what is!

So, in summary of this "second commandment" how would these verses be interpreted in the Sinner's Charter? Worship abounds in our culture, whether of flesh and blood, or inanimate objects, even ideas or fictitious characters. As "consumers" it is just a feature of the open market and the freedom of choice that is offered to us citizens. The idea of worshipping an invisible Being who, in many people's eyes, represents the "best forgotten" past, is an anathema, even though this "Being" happens to be the very Person Who gave us all life, sustains us and ultimately determines the years of our life, then judges us in terms of our *final destination.*

Around 33% of the world are Christian, 24% follow Islam, 15% are Hindus, 7% Buddhist and about 5% follow other religions. This leaves 16% unaccounted for, the *non-religious.* So, the third highest ranking "religion" in the world is not one with traditional beliefs, yet it is still a faith system, with objects of worship. We all believe in something, though many are in denial of this simple fact and where there is belief there is worship. People may deny belief in God but they are quite free in their entreaties to "dame fortune", fate, destiny, chance or luck (more of these in the next chapter). They have faith that their bodies will remain functioning, that the shops are still well-stocked, that the Earth continues to spin on its axis. They worship anything that gets them through the day, usually in the realm of entertainment in our "celebrity culture". We can't help it. Here is how I explained it in *The (other) "F" Word*, in a section where God is explaining Himself:

Ask yourselves why the ardent atheists out there are so sure that I don't exist that they are happy to spend a large part of their lives telling this to all who are happy to listen to them. As with every other human being, they have this unconscious desire to be connected to me. Let us call this the Longing. But their life journey has marred this desire. Perhaps they have been let down by one of my followers, or have parents who deny my existence, or maybe they just haven't been paying attention. They still have the Longing but instead of recognising its source they satisfy it in their own way with science, philosophy, politics or any other human endeavour born from the mind of man. The Longing has been redirected, as it has by all who answer it with products of their own cleverness, or even with the claims of rival gods.

Hating God has consequences, but loving Him produces unbounded joy. How deluded our society has become:

The god of this age has blinded the minds of unbelievers, so that they cannot see the light of the gospel that displays the glory of Christ, who is the image of God. (2 Corinthians 4:4).

The image of God is all that matters, but the World is blinded to this fact and, instead, offers us a whole gallery of substitute "images" to worship, as long as we don't break the rules of polite society! So here's a suggestion for our Sinner's charter:

Feel free to place your affections and favour anywhere you like, as long as you don't hurt or disrespect anyone. Whatever decision you make is yours and yours only and it is not up to anyone else to pass judgement on your choices.

God forgive them, for they know not what they do.

Mind your language

4

"You shall not misuse the name of the LORD your God, for the LORD will not hold anyone guiltless who misuses his name". (Exodus 20:7).

So what does this command, the third "commandment", mean by *misusing* God's Name? The JPS (official Jewish) translation translates it as taking the Name of God in a *vain oath*. Is this about taking oaths, or making solemn promises in His Name? The *Sefer ha-Chinuch* is a medieval Spanish commentary on the *Torah*, specifically the 613 laws and instructions within it. It interprets a vain oath as a trivial or unthinking misuse of God's Holy Name.

One example would be concerning issues that are patently impossible, such as swearing that a black object is in fact white. Or swearing on an issue that is patently obvious, such as insisting that a black object is actually black! An equally ridiculous vain oath would be to swear about something that is humanly impossible, such as flying without wings or going without sleep for a month. These are indeed ridiculous examples and it's hard to believe that God's Name would be used in such a way, that the Name above all Names would be used in such a trivial manner. Yet we see this in our everyday language, when we use His Name in such a throw-away way.

Rabbinical commentators had much to say about this commandment, because of the reverence they had for God's Name and the irreverence behind its misuse. One commentary declared that one who takes His Name in vain is to be considered as evil as an idol worshipper, because a reverence for God implies that His Name would never be used frivolously in an oath. This is not to say that God's Name couldn't be used in an oath, but rather that it couldn't be used *frivolously*. Those who do are surely playing with fire. In the *Midrash* we read of the Hasmonean King, Alexander Yannai, who apparently lost two thousand cities for too much swearing on oath. This was despite never swearing falsely, he simply over-used the process, with many of his oaths unnecessary!

Of course, in the New Testament, we are discouraged from this activity point-blank:

"Again, you have heard that it was said to the people long ago, 'Do not break your oath, but fulfill to the Lord the vows you have made.' But I tell you, do not swear an oath at all: either by heaven, for it is God's throne; or by the earth, for it is his footstool; or by Jerusalem, for it is the city of the Great King. And do not swear by your head, for you cannot make even one hair white or black. All you need to say is simply 'Yes' or 'No'; anything beyond this comes from the evil one." (Matthew 5:33-37).

And, again …

Above all, my brothers and sisters, do not swear—not by heaven or by earth or by anything else. All you need to say is a simple "Yes" or "No." Otherwise you will be condemned. (James 5:12).

We have a name for taking God's Name in vain, *blasphemy*. The *Torah* took this seriously. Breaking this commandment had consequences:

Say to the Israelites: 'If anyone curses his God, he will be held responsible; anyone who blasphemes the name of the LORD must be put to death. The entire assembly must stone him. Whether an alien or native-born, when he blasphemes the Name, he must be put to death'. (Leviticus 24:15-16).

It's as well we are not under the Old Covenant in terms of *consequences* of actions, otherwise the world would be a very lonely place, inhabited only by a few maiden aunts and the odd vicar, because the rest of us would have been stoned to death for blasphemy!

But I've never taken the name of God in vain in any way! Yes you have.

First, a list of some euphemisms for "God"; *by gad, oh my gosh, by gum, by Jove, by George, so 'elp me Bob, by Godfrey, great Scott, good grief, goodness gracious, begorrah*, we've all uttered one or two of these in our time, haven't we?

Then we have these; *Gadzooks* (God's hooks), *drat!* (God rot), *doggone* (God damn), *cor blimey* (God blind me), *by golly* (God's body), *darnation* (damnation), *strewth* (God's truth), *suffering succotash* (Suffering Saviour), *zounds* (God's wounds).

Then there are the alternative names for "Jesus"; *Jiminy Cricket, Gee wiz, Jeez, Gee, Jeepers, Judas Priest, Jeepers Creepers.*

For "Christ"; *Criminy, Crickey, Cripes, for crying out loud, chrissakes.*

For "Lord"; *Lor, Lawdy, Lumme* (Lord love me).

These are known as *minced oaths*, religious euphemisms that were created to avoid direct blasphemy, which in older days, would have got you in trouble with the authorities. Many of these would have been created round the time of the Puritans, who were particularly hot on this issue. Here's a typical notice from 1623:

For as much as all profane Swearing and Cursing is forbidden by the Word of GOD, be it therefore enacted, by the Authority of the then Parliament, that no Person or Persons should from thenceforth profanely Swear or Curse, upon Penalty of forfeiting one Shilling to the use of the Poor for every Oath or Curse. Refusal or inability to pay resulted in the offender being set in the stocks (if over twelve years old) or whipped if younger.

Have we taken the Lord's name in vain? Of course we have, though, in mitigation, we mostly haven't realised it, or have felt safe in the knowledge that a *derivation is not the actual word, so no worries!* I wonder what God thinks?

Yet even Christians have been known to utter such epithets as "Oh my God!" or "Oh God". These may not be seen as blasphemies, but perhaps can be suggested as over-familiarity with the Deity. The use of the phrase "Jesus Christ!" in all of its derivations seems to be on the rise in popular dramas, even our daytime soaps. We don't need euphemisms or *minced oaths* these days as there is no guilty conscience or penalties in uttering blasphemies. That's a good indication that our society today is very much *Post-Christian*.

It is revealing that blasphemy laws in England were originally underpinned by the declaration that *they were needed to uphold the national law, which is based on Christianity and that anything that targets Christianity is targeting the very foundation of England.* This, I believe, is a prophetic statement as the removal of these laws is surely concrete evidence of targeting Christianity, the very foundation of England. Times have changed and, in many cases, transformation of our culture has been subtle, like the proverbial slowly boiling frog, unaware of his gradual demise.

Evidence for this can be seen in the changing views of acceptable behaviour and language in that good old staple of our entertainment culture, the *sitcom*. To be specific, it is interesting to observe this in terms of attitudes to God and attitudes to 'victim groups', namely 'foreigners', women and the gay community. In short, until the 1980s, 'victim groups' were considered fair game. We had "Curry and Chips" with Spike Milligan blacked up as a Pakistani, "Til Death Us Do Part", with the racist anti-Semite (though the actor, Warren Mitchell was Jewish) Alf Garnett, "Are You Being Served?" with its stock gay character ("I'm free, Mr Rumbold!") and sexual innuendos, "Fawlty Towers", with Basil hating just about everyone and so on. Then came the 1980s with Ben Elton and left-leaning young comedians, bringing in the era of 'Alternative comedy'.

So what was alternative about it? There was a conscious effort to move away from the sexist and racist norms of British comedy, even though there was an innocence in the innuendo of those early sitcoms and, in many cases, the racism was actually poking fun at the instigators, such as Alf Garnett, who tended to be flawed and pitiful characters. What we received in its place was a perfect parallel to the changes in society. It now became offensive to disrespect perceived 'victim groups', but in its place crept in a far greater and insidious offence. Sitcoms now wouldn't dare poke fun at multiculturalism or the LGBT community but, instead, concentrate on pushing back the barriers of decency, in the name of 'progressiveness', in both words and behaviour. For example, the "F" word (only heard twice on TV in the 60s) is now commonplace and the "C" word has crept in (unthinkable even just a handful of years ago), but the "N" word would result in resignations and de-commissionings. Innocent sexual innuendo has given way to full nudity, simulated sex acts and detailed verbal expositions of the same. And, as for blasphemy, it is correct to say that "Jesus Christ" as an expletive is firmly embedded in the vocabulary of our entertainment landscape. Christian attitudes and lifestyle are regularly poked fun at and any "Christian" sitcom character is going to be judgemental, devious, untrustworthy, hypocritical or worse. And the sad thing is that, as we saw in the previous chapter, our society 'worships' that which is fed to it through the media. So out of the window goes any discernment or realisation of the rapidly diminishing standards of our culture.

The last person to be sent to prison for blasphemy in the UK was John Gott in 1921, who received nine months hard labour for publishing satirical pamphlets mocking Jesus. In 1949, Lord Denning said that "*it was thought that a denial of Christianity was liable to shake the fabric of society, which was itself founded upon Christian religion. There is no such danger to society now and the offence of blasphemy is a dead letter*". Could this be because our society has lost the fear of God? It seems so, especially when we remember the outrage from Christians at the broadcasting of the highly blasphemous "Jerry Springer: The Opera" at the BBC. Over 63,000 official complaints were made. The Christian group, *Christian Voice*, sought a private prosecution against the BBC on this matter. This was in fact the last attempted prosecution under the Blasphemy Laws in the UK and it failed on a technicality in that the laws did not cover theatre productions or media broadcasts! Another indicator of how our society today is *Post-Christian*.

So, moving on to another aspect of our speech, the use of certain words in common parlance. Read on …

The world is not as mysterious as it once was. Until our scientific age started digging away at the foundations, God was very much seen at the centre of all aspects of life. Of course, this may have led us into making incorrect conclusions about the mechanisms that control our lives and our world, but they got it right in that God is still *very much at the centre of our lives.* Here's a good example. Strokes these days kill or disadvantage thousands of people. It is described as a rapid loss of brain function due to the lack of blood reaching it. Of course we know that now, but we haven't always known that. In fact the word itself comes from the phrase, "a stroke of God's hand", attributing a divine cause to the condition. Interesting and curiously apt, as God has His hand on every aspect of our lives, whether we choose to believe this or not.

If I rise on the wings of the dawn, if I settle on the far side of the sea, even there your hand will guide me, your right hand will hold me fast. (Psalm 139:9-10).

After all, don't doctors still say, as both a comfort and an admission that they have done all they can, according to their knowledge, *"It's in God's hands now"*? They probably don't mean what they say, but that doesn't diminish the power of the concept.

Now there's another set of words that we use all of the time that tend to make me feel very uncomfortable. Here are a few sentences that illustrate this:

You're a lucky man! How fortunate you are! What are the chances?

We've all said these things, they are so tightly knitted in our everyday banter. Yet, when we look at the origin of these words …

Fortuna was the Roman goddess of luck, fate and fortune and the daughter of the chief god, *Jupiter.* She had temples dedicated to her and owned the *wheel of fortune* (now a TV game show), that she spun randomly to determine the fate of individuals. If you are *fortunate,* then Dame Fortune is surely smiling at you. A *lucky* person is surely in league with Lady Luck!

What are we really saying when we use these words? Is there a sense of invoking these pagan deities or at least acknowledging the power behind what seems to be random forces? Or is it a load of old nonsense and we shouldn't worry about it?

The next time you accidently hit your thumb with a hammer, meditate for a moment before your exclamation (as if!). Here are a few options you have that don't involve blasphemy or obscenity: *oh dear, deary me, ouch, that hurts!* Controversially, it may even be "spiritually correct" to utter a quick *f****, *s**** or *b********, rather than taking the Lord's name in vain.

Which brings us to our Sinner's Charter. How does the World view this "commandment"? I would suggest the following:

We must learn to respect each other in words as well as actions, so we must be careful how we speak, otherwise we may be (perhaps unwittingly) committing an offence against society and be dealt with accordingly.

Rest and Peace

"Remember the Sabbath day by keeping it holy. Six days you shall labor and do all your work, but the seventh day is a sabbath to the LORD your God. On it you shall not do any work, neither you, nor your son or daughter, nor your male or female servant, nor your animals, nor any foreigner residing in your towns. For in six days the LORD made the heavens and the earth, the sea, and all that is in them, but he rested on the seventh day. Therefore the LORD blessed the Sabbath day and made it holy." (Exodus 20:8-11).

This is a biggie, for two reasons. For a start, it is the longest "commandment" uttered, as you remember, from the very Mouth of God, which indicates that perhaps it has special significance for Him. Secondly, it's the only "commandment" that Christians *really get into a flap about.* Is it just for Jews? What about Jews who follow Jesus? What about Gentile Christians? What about everybody else?

So we have four separate categories, the only "commandment" that we add conditions to. Perhaps we are looking at this the wrong way? Perhaps there is one universal truth here and we are missing it? There is, I believe a story to be told here and tell it I will ... eventually. But first ...

The first word, in Hebrew, is different when we compare Exodus 20 with the corresponding passage in Deuteronomy 5. Let's look at the verses in question.

Remember the Sabbath day by keeping it holy. (Exodus 20:8).

Observe the Sabbath day by keeping it holy, as the **LORD** *your God has commanded you.* (Deuteronomy 5:12).

The Exodus word is *zakar*, meaning remember, recall or call to mind. The Deuteronomy word is *shamar*, meaning observe, keep or guard. There's a subtle difference between these words. The rabbis suggest that the first is a positive command, to encourage us to perform good acts on the Sabbath and that the second is a negative command, warning us against desecrating the Sabbath. Some of them go on to suggest that both commands were uttered at exactly the same time, emphasising the equal importance of both. This gives every impression of being a major deal with God. Why would this be?

Let's face it, the first three "commandments" are explicitly descriptive of the needs of God's determination that we should not be led astray by "other gods", nor worship substitutes, nor blaspheme Him. Yet this fourth "commandment" doesn't seem to be as personal in our way of thinking. *But perhaps we are mistaken in this and the Sabbath is far dearer to God than we imagine!*

Here is some evidence for this thinking.

1. God spent more time on this "commandment" than any other and felt the need to re-iterate the Scripture where it was first mentioned. (Genesis 2:2-3).

2. Sabbath is the first thing that God made holy. (Genesis 2:3).

3. Jesus re-iterates the other "commandments" (mainly in Mark 10:17-18) but is silent on the Sabbath in

the sense that he never declared *"You shall keep the Sabbath …"*. The Church has interpreted this silence in a negative sense, that Jesus obviously didn't agree that it should continue. Yet he obviously observed it (in its truest sense, rather than how the Pharisees kept it e.g. Matthew 12:9-11). Also, why then would he warn the people concerning the end times, how hard it would be if the bad events occurred on a Sabbath (Matthew 24:19-21). Surely this is an argument for the *continuation of the Sabbath even up to the Last Days?*

4. In my experience I have discovered that issues that cause the greatest confusion and upsets in the Church are usually the issues that are closest to God's heart. I wrote about a few of these in my book, *How the Church Lost the Truth,* calling them "battlegrounds", where Greek thinking has created havoc in our understanding of the things of God. These were Creation, Israel, Hell, Salvation and End Times. I would now, formally, choose to add the *Sabbath* to this list.

5. He was teaching us something very special about this day, something that is not just concerned with obeying a "commandment" but something that was going to benefit us. Let's explore this further …

Let's start with Jesus himself:

Then he said to them, "The Sabbath was made for man, not man for the Sabbath. So the Son of Man is Lord even of the Sabbath." (Mark 2:27-28).

If Jesus was Lord even of the Sabbath, doesn't that imply that it still had relevance, just like everything else Jesus was Lord over, otherwise he would have added such words as, *and anyway it has no meaning for you now that I am here?*

So, Biblically, there is nothing explicitly suggesting that God has done away with the Sabbath, so the *function* remains the same, even if the *form* may change. What do I mean by that? The function of the Sabbath is to *provide a time of rest:*

By the seventh day God had finished the work he had been doing; so on the seventh day he rested from all his work. Then God blessed the seventh day and made it holy, because on it he rested from all the work of creating that he had done. (Genesis 2:2-3).

Even Christians, whether Jew or Gentile, are reminded of the function of the Sabbath:

There remains, then, a Sabbath-rest for the people of God; for anyone who enters God's rest also rests from their works, just as God did from his. Let us, therefore, make every effort to enter that rest, so that no one will perish by following their example of disobedience. (Hebrews 4:9-11).

The function remains the same and that really is the major point. This is what I think God is saying to us in the "fourth commandment":

If I left you to your own devices, you'd all get so wrapped up in your own lives you'd miss so many blessings I have for you. By obeying the Sabbath together as one people on one day you will be able to appreciate these blessings in a holy place in time and space, where you can appreciate your loved ones, the Creation that surrounds you and enjoy uninterrupted fellowship with me. It's what Adam and Eve once had and it's a foretaste of what I have prepared for you for that day when all will be made right and good.

It's so good when we read it like this, no wonder we have messed it up. It's as if mankind has decided that it doesn't deserve it. We have made it into a controversy, a divisive thing, a religious hot-potato. Even some who celebrate it have over-complicated it with added extras and exclusivist attitudes. Let's see what the Rabbis have done with it.

... by keeping it holy.

What was probably meant as just a verbal proclamation to usher in the Sabbath, has become a *sanctification* over wine, with benedictions to ring-fence it from the rest of the week. This was to be a day when one dresses, eats and drinks differently as if entertaining a bride! In terms of what one does during that period, there are numerous interpretations.

In terms of *rest* this is not necessarily interpreted as lounging around doing nothing, but rather a time dedicated to God, with great spiritual activity, the reading of Scripture and marvelling over the wonders of Creation, with a carefulness over thoughts, words and actions.

In terms of prohibited work it gets more interesting. It appears that the original list is based on the thirty-nine activities engaged on, when building the original Tabernacle in the wilderness. It has since been expanded on and covers such oddities as lighting a match, turning on (or off) anything electrical, moving vases (unless using an elbow) or leaving your house with gum in your mouth.

There seems to be one exception that cuts through all the red tape and exposes the beating heart of an understanding of God's ways. It is *pikuach nefesh*, the saving of a life, a basic rule that trumps all others, even the Sabbath laws. The idea is that one should live by *Torah* rules rather than die because of them!

For in six days the LORD made the heavens and the earth, the sea, and all that is in them, but he rested on the

seventh day. Therefore the LORD blessed the Sabbath day and made it holy. (Exodus 20:11).

Here we have the basic reason for the Sabbath spelled out and the clue is in the original Hebrew, not in the English translation, though the KJV, strangely enough, is closest. The first part of the verse, in Hebrew, reads as follows:

For six days ....

The KJV compromises with *"For (in) six days ..."* The issue is that the prefix "in" is not present in the Hebrew and the implication is that God didn't just create the heavens and the earth, but also the six days ... *time itself!* And the Sabbath was to be the pinnacle of this creation. That is why He blessed it and made it holy. So, recognising Sabbath is to recognise God as Creator. This is a thought worth holding on to. We cannot help but come to the conclusion, as Bible believers, that *there is something very special about the Sabbath.*

Which makes it so sad that the institutional Church has never accepted this fact and has done all that it can to distance itself from God's own sentiments about this day. Here's what the church did (a summary of the relevant chapter in my book, *Shalom*):

We begin with the official proclamation of Emperor Constantine, the man who created the concept of Christendom, with Christianity as the official religion of the Roman Empire. Here's his first proclamation regarding the change of Sabbath, in AD 321: "On the venerable Day of the Sun let the magistrates and people residing in cities rest, and let all workshops be closed."

This was made a lot more official in AD 364, with

the proclamation (Canon 29) of the Council of Laodicea: "Christians shall not Judaize and be idle on Saturday but shall work on that day; but the Lord's day they shall especially honour, and, as being Christians, shall, if possible, do no work on that day. If, however, they are found Judaizing, they shall be shut out from Christ."

What do we conclude from this? Firstly, that the instigation of the change of the "Sabbath" was political and born out of the "Christian" anti-Semitism that was endemic to "Christendom". Secondly, that the initial intention was to emulate the mechanism of the Sabbath through enforcement. If this is no different to what the Jewish people are urged to do on a Sabbath, then we are simply moving the Sabbath from Saturday to Sunday. I would suggest that there is something different going on here, culminating in an artificial construct, not prompted by Scripture, but rather by man.

The Church of Constantine was one born out of political expediency. After all, if Christianity was going to be the official religion of the Roman Empire, then it would effectively be the tool of the Roman Empire, in order to be able to rule the people effectively. And what better way was there to unify the Empire than to give them a set of ideas to believe in? The trouble is that Christianity itself wasn't unified, so his first task was to firm up a unified set of beliefs and then give firm instructions how these beliefs should be followed. All this was done at the council of Nicaea and out of this came the newly constructed churches and cathedrals, with a prescribed day, the Sunday – the existing pagan day for communal worship – to practice their "Christianity".

If this new "religion" of Christianity was to be an effective tool for the State, then it needed to realise that it had to abide by the State's rules. It suited Constantine and those who followed to declare to the people that their only religious obligations were to attend Church on a Sunday and try to abstain from work that day. Thus was born the Sunday "Sabbath", a day that has retained this prescribed function right up to today.

So what of today? Having accepted that, for all intents and purposes, the "Sabbath" is now on a Sunday, it is sad to see the creeping secularisation that has been eating away at any intention of this day being special. In the 1994 Sunday Trading act the only restrictions imposed were that larger shops could open only for six continual hours and that they should close on Easter Sunday. Our local high street, frankly, is busier on a Sunday than any other days of the week. What has happened to the Sabbath then? More importantly, what has happened to the *idea* of the Sabbath?

Secularists and progressives would see it as some form of a triumph to wrench Sunday away from religious restrictions. But what have they actually achieved by doing this? Christian campaigning group *Keep Sunday Special!* have commented on the effect that current (and proposed) Sunday trading laws has had on various sectors of society. For families it would be less time that they would have together, with 77% of poll respondents from parents suggesting that work already impinges too much on family life. Unions have reported on the significant damage to work-life balance of workers, and retailers have quoted statistics showing that no real long-term financial benefits have resulted from Sunday opening hours. It's the *function* of Sabbath that we must keep returning to, even if we remove the religious trappings. It is a *day of rest*. We need rest. We need time to take a breath, away from the rat-race, to enjoy friends and family. It's our society that sees us as economic units rather than human beings, as consumers rather than people. God saw all this coming, He reminds us continually through His eternal Word of the importance of rest, specifically a day of rest, preferably on the assigned day, the Saturday Sabbath but, if that isn't possible, *any day is better than no day!*

Incredibly (though we shouldn't be surprised), there is support from science, specifically from a new discipline called *chronobiology*, which examines biological rhythms in animals and human beings. There is a cercaseptan rhythm, that occurs every seven days, governing many biological functions, from chemical production to blood pressure to heartbeat. This is a young science, but one of its findings is that bees in Brazil observe a sabbath rest every seven days and that creatures that align with this seven day cycle live longer! Also the *Seventh Day Adventists* claim that, statistically, they live seven years longer than the average person. Well, they would say that, though I have yet to see the evidence. Nevertheless, none of this is inconsistent with a loving God who provides us with specific commands for good, healthy living, so we should be hugely encouraged by these scientific discoveries.

Our *Sinner's Charter* would have this to say about the fourth commandment:

Work, rest and play. You have freedom to choose what works for you, but you also have a responsibility for your family and your sense of self-worth to be a good citizen and help support the economy. No day is extra special and no-one has the right to impose their ancient traditions on your daily life.

Family really matters

6

"Honour your father and your mother, so that you may live long in the land the LORD your God is giving you." (Exodus 20:12).

On the face of it we have moved from viewing God-centred "commandments" to those concerned with how we get on with our fellow human beings. Some would argue otherwise. They would suggest that, at the very least, this fifth "commandment" is a bridge between God-centred rules and man-centred rules. They would insist that, although the wording seems to place it firmly within a human framework, it is very clearly more about our relationship with God than we perhaps realise.

The thinking is that there are three agencies working together to produce every human being; a mother, a father and God Himself. So, to honour your parents is also to honour He who is present in the process and to dishonour them is to dishonour Him too. This commandment has an extra emphasis in the Deuteronomy version:

"Honour your father and your mother, **as the LORD your God has commanded you ..."** (Deuteronomy 5:16).

To honour your parents is a Divine imperative with no ulterior motive. It's not to sweeten them up for a good inheritance or to gain favour in the family pecking order, or even out of sentimentality or moral obligation. We honour our parents, even if they don't have two pennies to rub together, or if they favour a sibling, or are thoroughly bad eggs, undeserving of your love. We do it *because God has commanded us.* They brought you into this world, they gave you life. Even if the subsequent years weren't exactly a bed of roses, *you still honour them* and this gratitude is to give you great credit and something that God will not forget. There is a similar command in Leviticus:

'Each of you must respect your mother and father ... '
(Leviticus 19:3).

Notice the word order. We honour our father first, then our mother, but we *respect* our mother first, then our father. This is significant, nothing is random in Hebrew Scripture, word orders are very important. The rabbis suggest that we tend to *honour* our mothers more than our fathers because of our mother's nurturing role in our upbringing, in contrast with the father's role in admonishment and punishment. They also suggest that we tend to respect our fathers more than our mothers, possibly out of fear. For this reason, we must *honour* our father first, as it may not come naturally to us and likewise, we must *respect* our mother first.

There is a consequence stated in the verse, *so that you may live long in the land the LORD your God is giving you.* One presumes that this can work both ways, either as a promise (if you are honourable)... or a curse (if you are dishonourable)! So what does this mean in its original context? Is this a magical formula for long life? All you have to do is look after your old parents to the end and then you get your reward? If this was what God intended then we would all be doing it, perhaps through gritted teeth ... *all for the wrong reasons!* Apparently, the original context was an Ancient Near Eastern legal necessity, where children would only inherit their parent's property if they honoured them properly by looking after them in their old age. More insights can be gleaned by again looking at the longer version of the commandment, in Deuteronomy 5:16:

... so that you may live long **and that it may go well with you** *in the land the LORD your God is giving you.*

The extra words here are in bold above. There are various rabbinical explanations for this addition. Some rabbis say that it's an extra assurance to those who saw Moses break the first tablets of stone and would fear the removal of the long life that was promised. Also, it has been noticed that the second version has seventeen extra Hebrew letters, which is the numerical equivalent of the word for "goodness", again intended as an extra assurance.

In summary we see here the importance of the biological and spiritual relationships that comprise the structure of a basic family. Father and mother coming together biologically to create the next generation in collaboration with Our spiritual Creator who:

... created my inmost being; you knit me together in my mother's womb. (Psalm 139:13).

... made you, who formed you in the womb. (Isaiah 44:2).

... before I formed you in the womb I knew you. (Jeremiah 1:5).

This is the context of the basic family structure, as referenced in the "Ten Commandments". But what of today? What of the "Sinner's Charter"? For instance, does it demand that we honour our parents? We now live in a world where the concept of *family* is not as straightforward as it once was. Here is a passage on the Wikipedia page for "history of the family":

"There were two distinct family patterns that emerged in Christian Europe throughout the Middle Ages. In most of Southern and Eastern Europe, marriage occurred between two individuals who had lived with their parents for a long period of time. The man involved was older, usually in his late twenties, and the girl was often still a teenager. Their household would contain several generations, an occurrence demographers denote as a "complex" household. In contrast, areas in Northwestern Europe gave rise to a familial structure that was unique for the time period. The man and woman were typically around the same age, and would wait until they were in their early twenties to marry. Following the marriage, the couple would set up their own independent household (termed a "nuclear" household structure). This led to a lower birthrate, as well as greater levels of economic stability for the new couple. This also served as a check on the increasing population in Europe. Many women in this region during this time period would never marry at all."

This is an interesting observation. The first pattern is the one perhaps closest to the Biblical ideal, with households functioning as mini-clans, cramming together many generations into one home. This has certainly been the Jewish model up to current times. Here's a snippet of how I described it in *"Shalom"*, in the chapter on *Mishpocha*.

The key concept with mishpocha is that it is not the nuclear family of 2.4 children that we have been brought up with, but the extended family that includes grandparents, uncles, aunts and cousins, where the cooking pot is in permanent use, where

the atmosphere jangles with human voices, cries,
prayers and laughter, where caring and sharing
crosses the generations. This has become an utterly
alien concept to most of us these days. We strive for
our own space, we crave personal expression.
Community has been replaced by individuality as
we disengage our lives from people and replace
them with stuff, such as consumer electronics,
furniture and objets d'art. Stuff doesn't answer
back, stuff doesn't have demands, stuff doesn't need
looking after.

But stuff doesn't look after you when you're
poorly, stuff doesn't go that extra mile for you, stuff
doesn't love you. Mishpocha ensures that the
wisdom and stories of your grandparents are not
lost, mishpocha celebrates family occasions as
extended times of joy and sharing, mishpocha
provides an endless supply of babysitters, household
operatives and shoulders to cry on. Mishpocha
means you never need to be lonely, though it could
also potentially be stifling and claustrophobic.
Mishpocha, though, does require a big house.

Mishpocha is most accurately defined as 'the
entire family network of relatives by blood or
marriage (and sometimes close friends)', so in its
widest definition it is talking about a small
community, united either by blood or friendship, or
in a Christian sense, by conviction (or, in fact, all
three). Church families ought to be mishpocha, but
with that added divine ingredient that ensures
relationships are vertical as well as horizontal.

Of course, as described in the Wikipedia article, we
now generally follow the Northwestern Europe model,

... Following the marriage, the couple would set up their own independent household (termed a "nuclear" household structure). This led to a lower birthrate, as well as greater levels of economic stability for the new couple ...

This is also becoming the norm in secular Jewish families, as well as in other communities, such as Asian and African, who live among us in our multicultural melting-pot. The lure of economic stability has generally trumped the need for traditional multi-generational family structures and sons and daughters have flown the nest to set up home wherever career prospects are maximised. But the "downsizing" trend continues, fuelled by the individualism of our age. More and more people are now choosing to live alone or as couples with no children, the nuclear family is becoming a quieter place, perhaps as electronic gadgets take the place of flesh and blood. In the UK, the number of people living in family homes with kids fell from 52% in 1961 to 36% in 2009, no doubt even lower now.

It's been a downward trend, a shrinking of families from double figures, to single figures, to a solitary person in a bedsit surrounded by a virtual family brought to their electronic screens through social media. In this context, how does the fifth "commandment" hold up? Are we honouring our parents less by distancing ourselves geographically from them?

Let's first view some statistics from *Age UK*, concerning issues for the elderly in the UK.

- One million pensioners in the UK live in severe poverty.
- £3.8 billion in benefits for old people goes unclaimed every year.

- 37% of older people who are not online are unaware that advice is available.
- Nearly 1000 older people are admitted to hospital daily for trivial reasons.
- Only about a third of people aged 50 and over think that older people who receive care services are treated with dignity and respect.

These statistics seem to point to a lot of elderly people who are being let down. We usually use the phrase 'let down by the system' but then we have to ask, *what is the system?* Is it the State's responsibility to be the primary carers for our elderly ... *or their own sons and daughters?*

Of course, as the family statistics already indicated, families are shrinking and there's a good chance many of these elderly folk won't have children. But many will, so *what has happened to honouring our father and mother?*

With the 'original model', with parents living close by their children or even in the same house, primary care is not an issue. Even though there may be State involvement, it would be at the children's initiative. But in our new 'western model', can there not be a hint of, *out of sight out of mind?* Children who have done well financially may well be happy to forgo their inheritance and be unconcerned to see it channelled into the pockets of a care home. They possibly feel their consciences are salved and that an occasional visit to the 'old 'uns' would be the sum total of their responsibility. Is this honouring their parents? Of course, this is a can of worms as there will be children, because of circumstances, unable to honour their parents in the way they would like. What I am looking at here is the 'bigger picture' in our modern society of the ease with which many children would hand their parents over to the State for their welfare in their 'latter years'. Once we give the State control of our parents, then we find ourselves in a very different environment, with a very different moral framework than if we were nurturing them within the extended family home. Here are a couple of worrying facts:

- The wholesale drugging of the elderly in both private and public nursing homes has reached epidemic levels, with the use of anti-psychotics, anti-anxiety drugs (tranquilizers) and antidepressants. Patients are being harmed and their lives cut short as a direct result.

    These drugs are highly dangerous when prescribed to anyone, but when prescribed to the elderly the risks for diabetes, stroke and sudden death are greatly increased.

    (Citizens Commission on Human Rights UK).

- Surveys suggest most UK doctors support legal assisted dying, and most people want it. A series of articles published by The BMJ today, explore the debate around assisted dying, in which, subject to safeguards, terminally ill people who are near to death, suffering, and of sound mind, could ask for drugs that they would take to end their lives …

    Jacky Davis, Consultant Radiologist at the Whittington Hospital in London, points to a recent survey showing that most UK doctors support legislation for assisted dying, while a 2015 poll showed that about 80% of the UK public support a change in the law. Yet the BMA, which represents UK doctors, has long been opposed to assisted dying, despite calls for it to adopt a neutral stance.

    (British Medical Journal).

"Honour your father and your mother ..."

Before we round this up, we need to be aware that honouring parents is not just an activity we do when they are most needy i.e. when they are old and dependent. There is no time marker on this command. We need to honour them at all stages of our relationship with them, whether as a dependent child or an independent adult. We need to give them the respect they deserve purely through who they are. We may think that they don't need our respect, in fact we may mostly take them for granted, but they will always deserve our respect, because that is what the Commandment implores us to do.

We return to the basic message. Society has changed enormously since Bible times. Community living has given way to narrower horizons, driven by the individualism that encourages us to live lives of personal ambition and to pursue happiness. Subtle indoctrination of humanistic philosophy has assured us that the *State knows best* and *your conscience is clear, hand over your burdens to us.* Of course, there will be scenarios, perhaps where you simply don't have the space, time or resources, when you are forced to rely on the NHS or private care homes. But the point being made here is a general one, not a specific one. Our society encourages the fragmentation of community, particularly multi-generation family living. Go west young man ... and seek your fortune. So, it is up to us all individually to decide, given our particular circumstance, whether we are honouring our parents or not. More so for Christians who are still bound by the fifth commandment, to examine their consciences before God and decide whether they are truly giving honour in the way that God would want them to.

By way of contrast, The Sinner's Charter would probably read something like this:

Do what seems best for your parents, at all times, but rest assured that society can ease the burden of an aged relative, so trust it to look after your loved ones in a satisfactory manner.

The Killing fields

"You shall not murder". (Exodus 20:13).

It has been disclosed that sex-selective abortions may have resulted in the deaths of more than twenty-three million girls around the world. Research from the National University of Singapore, reported in the New Scientist, found that, since sex-selective abortion became readily available in the 1970s, male births dominated in twelve countries. The majority of "missing" females are in China and India, with the deaths more or less equally split between the two. Is it right to call these "deaths"? If so, then surely this is murder on an apocalyptic scale, yet nobody has been brought to book over it.

Have you seen some of the videos on what actually happens with some late abortions and the tools that are employed to perform these procedures? It is beyond horrific and on a par with images of gruesome atrocities that emerge from human conflicts. Out of sight, out of mind?

Just a few inches of female flesh separate the killing fields of the womb from the incubator in intensive care. And the former situation is triggered by a single decision, that of the mother whether to abort the foetus, for whatever reason. A chilling comparison is to those Roman emperors who controlled the lives of defeated gladiators simply through the swivel of a fist and a protruding thumb. This is not to put the basic morality of the mother on par with this Roman gruesomeness, simply to examine the moral climate that makes such decisions possible. It is society and its laws that are in the dock here, whether or not a foetus has the right to live and whether the mother has a right to choose? Both questions are connected because, if a foetus has no right to live, then the mother is free to choose life or death and, conversely, if the foetus has the right to live, the mother has to think long and hard about the decision she is going to make.

Does a foetus have a right to live? Following my opening statement in the previous paragraph, is this governed by mere geography? Surely, in the short distance between womb and mother's breast, nothing has changed physically, spiritually or morally for that "baby-to-be"? Early in 2019 in the USA, the Republicans put forward a bill called the *Born-Alive Abortion Survivors Protection Act*. Its aim was to ensure that, in the case where aborted babies survive, doctors provide as much care in the well-being of the baby than if it had been a normal birth. Thanks to opposition by some Democrats, the bill was defeated! What does this say about (some in) society's view on whether a foetus has a right to live?

Is abortion murder? You decide.

"You shall not murder."

In the *Melchita* (Jewish writings) it was said that God etched the "Ten Commandments" so that the second group of five matched the first group of five. Consequently, the sixth "commandment", *you shall not murder*, was a reflection of the first, *I Am the Lord your God*. So, anyone who sheds blood is as if they have marred the Divine likeness, as we are all made in the Image of God. It was considered that serious.

The key Hebrew word is *retsach* and is mostly translated as "murder". Yet the King James Version (as well as the

American Standard Version) uses the word, "kill". The implication then for English-speaking Christians up to modern times was that every situation involving the taking of life is a breaking of this "commandment". The word "murder" is, of course, more nuanced and excuses situations of self-defence and war (inasmuch as 'the laws of war' are followed) but it is, as always, to the Bible that we turn to get further insight.

The Bible asserts that murder is *unlawful killing*. As already noted, God hates murder because we are all made in His image and likeness (Genesis 1:26-27, 9:4-6). Jesus also spoke out against murder:

"You have heard that it was said to the people long ago, 'You shall not murder, and anyone who murders will be subject to judgment.' But I tell you that anyone who is angry with a brother or sister will be subject to judgment." (Matthew 5:21-22).

Of course, Jesus broadens this to include those who are inclined towards taking their anger to the next stage. Paul adds his penny's worth:

Furthermore, just as they did not think it worthwhile to retain the knowledge of God, so God gave them over to a depraved mind, so that they do what ought not to be done. They have become filled with every kind of wickedness, evil, greed and depravity. They are full of envy, murder, strife, deceit and malice. (Romans 1:28-29).

As does James:

If you really keep the royal law found in Scripture, "Love your neighbor as yourself," you are doing right. But if you show favoritism, you sin and are convicted by the law as lawbreakers. For whoever keeps the whole law and yet stumbles at just one point is guilty of breaking all of it. For he who said, "You shall not commit adultery," also said, "You shall not murder." If you do not commit adultery but do commit murder, you have become a lawbreaker. (James 2:8-11).

In the Hebrew scriptures, the following constituted *lawful* killing:

- Punishment for murder (Exodus 21:12-36, Leviticus 24:17,21).

- Punishment for adultery (Leviticus 20:10, Deuteronomy 22:22-24).

- Warfare (Deuteronomy 20:1-20).

- Self-defence (Exodus 22:2-3).

Capital punishment (the death penalty) at the time of Moses was quite severe. Exodus 21 gives a long list of lawful killing. This includes punishment for intentional killing, attacking or cursing your parents, kidnapping or allowing your bull to kill someone. Deuteronomy 22 adds to the list matters of adultery and sexual deviancy. You can be killed for promiscuity, adultery and incest. Also to be put to death are sorceresses, those who commit bestiality, or who sacrifice to other gods. There are also other situations, not listed here, but the point has been made that Hebrew society was regulated by the death penalty for extreme misdemeanours.

Warfare provided exceptions to the rule, as we read in Deuteronomy 20. Killing in battle was positively encouraged, as long as God initiated the proceedings, when He even promised to be *the one who goes with you to fight for you.* There were even exemptions to excuse combat, such as newlyweds and the fearful and fainthearted (vs 5-9). Those who did battle were encouraged to be thorough, often encouraged to completely destroy the enemy (vs. 17).

Another exception is given in Exodus 22:2-3:

"If a thief is caught breaking in at night and is struck a fatal blow, the defender is not guilty of bloodshed; but if it happens after sunrise, the defender is guilty of bloodshed."

This tells us that the defender's act of self-defence was acceptable, unless the attack was in daylight, when presumably the defender has had time to assess the situation and that even the thief's life was considered so valuable to make such a death illegal.

But we are, of course, living in different times. Is life considered so much more valuable that capital punishment has been deemed unacceptable for every category of murder, whether the Bible considers it legal or illegal? The death penalty was abandoned in Great Britain in 1965, although fifty-six countries still practice it. In earlier days life was certainly considered cheap, cheap enough in Tudor times for King Henry VIII's reign to boast 72,000 executions, many of them for charges of heresy. Also, tens of thousands of women were executed as witches during the middle ages. In the 18th and early 19th Centuries the UK had a horrific system in operation called the *Bloody Code*, which featured 220 crimes punishable by death, including living with Gypsies for a month, stealing sheep or goods valued as low as 12 pence and using a disguise while committing a crime!

Reforms were in place since the start of the 20th Century and 1957 gave us the Homicide Act, which made a distinction between capital and non-capital murder. This resulted in just six categories of murder that were punishable by death; during a burglary, by shooting or causing an explosion, resisting arrest, killing a police officer, killing a prison officer and repeat offending. But this confused and divided the Nation and, in 1965, MP Sydney Silverman introduced a bill, passed by a free vote of 200 votes to 98, to abolish the death penalty.

Why have we abolished the death penalty? Is it that we are living in more enlightened times? During the last few judicial executions the questions being asked by the public, encouraged by the media were: did society have the right to take life at all? Were innocent people being hanged? Was hanging really the deterrent it had always been made out to be? Was hanging humane? As God was no longer at the centre of decision making in our society, the questions that were being asked were humanistic rather than justice-centred and seemed to be concerned more and more with the *rights of the perpetrator*, rather than the victim of the crime. We now face situations where unrepentant serial killers and mass murderers escape capital punishment where every bone of your body is crying, *justice for the victims, an eye for an eye* but the statute book urges mercy for these evil people. And we wonder why. They certainly would have been executed in a society run on Biblical principles.

"You shall not murder."

We must not forget that this refers to the original crime, rather than the justice meted out to the perpetrator, who would receive the ultimate judgement in both Old and New Testament days.

"Anyone who strikes a person with a fatal blow is to be put to death". (Exodus 21:12).

"You have heard that it was said to the people long ago, 'You shall not murder, and anyone who murders will be subject to judgment.' But I tell you that anyone who is

angry with a brother or sister will be subject to judgment." (Matthew 5:21-22)

As the New Testament is concerned with God's kingdom, rather than the Kingdom of the World, it was never meant to have the power to execute such judgements and the only place, I believe, in the New Testament where an extreme judgement was carried out (for a much more trivial offence) was God's judgement on Ananias and Sapphira (Acts 5:1-11).

Holland abolished the death penalty in 1870, but brought it back briefly in 1944 to execute wartime collaborators. It will even refuse to extradite criminals if there is a possibility that they would face a death penalty elsewhere. The Dutch government must have a very high value on human life. Really? It doesn't seem to have an issue with *euthanasia*, a word that they don't use, preferring the expression, *assisted suicide* and *termination of life on request*. Holland is a pioneer in this, ready to assist people of all ages and circumstances to end their lives but refusing to do the same, for the most evil of murderers. So, it's not death that concerns them it's the individual's freedom to live or die. If the individual seeks death then they will assist, if an individual deserves death then they will do anything but. But even this is changing, with a recent case in France where a quadriplegic patient had his life support systems switched off by the state, despite the wishes of his Catholic parents.

So, to answer a question posed earlier, *are we living in more enlightened times?* We are now living in a society wrenched from its Biblical roots which basically gives us rules by consensus, by what seems fair to us, in other words, *government by human wisdom.* If this means slaughtering millions of innocent pre-born babies without a tinge of conscience, or facilitating the deaths of those with suicidal tendencies, or preserving the life of those who have intentionally taken the lives of others ... *then so be it.* If that's progressive, or enlightened, then surely we must mourn the passing of more primitive times, when God's absolute laws governed our society ... if indeed these times ever existed!

The Sinner's Charter virtually writes itself on this issue:

You must not kill another regardless of the circumstances and seek to preserve life as society defines it, unless personal freedom compels you otherwise.

To have and to hold

"You shall not commit adultery." (Exodus 20:14).

The key word here is *na'aph* (commit adultery). It is primarily used in human terms in the sense of the betrayal within a marriage. But it also has spiritual connotations in the prophetic writings:

I gave faithless Israel her certificate of divorce and sent her away because of all her adulteries. Yet I saw that her unfaithful sister Judah had no fear; she also went out and committed adultery. (Jeremiah 3:8).

Consequences here were extreme as they were, in the previous chapter, for adultery of the fleshy variety.

"'If a man commits adultery with another man's wife— with the wife of his neighbor—both the adulterer and the adulteress are to be put to death'". (Leviticus 20:10).

Either way, God likes this not a bit! A further clue is given when we return to the Hebrew word, *na'aph*, which is a contraction of two words that give the meaning "make anger". The adulterer is in a select group that particularly arouses the great anger of God.

So I will come to put you on trial. I will be quick to testify against sorcerers, adulterers and perjurers, against those who defraud laborers of their wages, who oppress the widows and the fatherless, and deprive the foreigners among you of justice, but do not fear me," says the LORD Almighty. (Malachi 3:5).

Murder may be an attack on God in the sense of destroying the Image of God that is within us, but adultery scythes at the very heart of God's *covenant* with us, be it the marriage covenant or the one we make when we join the Kingdom of priests and become one of *His people*. Adultery arouses His Divine anger more than any other sin because of the disharmony it brings to relationships all around. Also, as we saw in the previous chapter, it was said that God etched the "Ten Commandments" so that the second group of five matched the first group of five. Consequently, the seventh "commandment", *you shall not commit adultery*, was a reflection of the second, you shall have no other gods before me. Spiritual adultery was and still is a serious business.

Adultery these days, in the sense of a betrayal of a marriage, is so commonplace as to be socially acceptable and certainly not the stuff of *gossip behind net curtains* as it would have been a generation ago. In a survey in *Divorce* magazine in 2018 it was noted that, in America, 45-50% of married women and 50-60% of married men cheat on their spouses and this accounts for around 30% of divorces. It was also stated that around 70% of couples stay together after an affair is discovered. This is a high figure but perhaps is a reflection of changing times, when marriage was once considered for life, *'til death us do part,* but is now mainly viewed as an optional extra in the game of life. God sees it far more seriously than we do (including some Christians). The level of Christian divorces, even without extenuating circumstances, is running almost as high as in the secular world.

Sex is seen these days as a 'divine right' for all, however one may indulge (within the law, of course). A telling indictment of the current licentious climate is illustrated by a poster I have just seen for HIV/Aids prevention. Here is the wording: *There are many ways to prevent HIV: having regular tests, using a condom, taking preventative drugs. Do it your way* ...

How about the only 100% proven way to have sex and avoid HIV? Abstinence or waiting for marriage? Not acceptable options these days as they impinge on our human right to pursue pleasure without consequence and so not an option in our 'brave new world'!

Adultery is seen as entertainment, with soap opera ratings spiking when there are saucy shenanigans on offer and lurid tabloid headlines showcasing the latest celebrity affair guaranteed to add a few million to the circulation. Just like young toddlers having to be instructed to do good, because naughtiness is so natural for them, the same goes for us adults; there's something about the breaking of marriage vows that piques our interest and sense of superiority. *Even celebrities / royalty / politicians are only human like the rest of us. What fun to see them suffer!* But God suffers too. This is because marriage is so important to Him.

There was a piece of news in 2017 that has been largely overlooked but, in the grand scheme of things, was significant. The Scottish wing of the Anglican Church had just voted to legalise gay marriage. After giving his reasons, the head of the Scottish Episcopal Church, David Chillingworth stated that *"we affirm we are a church of diversity and difference bound together by our unity in Christ"*. The Bishop of Edinburgh, John Armes, added, *"if the Anglican Communion is to survive it must embrace unity"*.

If Church unity demands that Biblical doctrine on marriage is thrown out of the window, then I suggest that the Anglican Communion does not deserve to survive, whatever the implications. In terms of core understandings of what a Church is in relation to Jesus, this doctrine is far more precious than these Scottish clergymen seem to understand, far more important than the survival of a single denomination, regardless of how many clergy it employs or the size of its investment portfolio.

To get things in perspective, let us go back to basics. Marriage has many forms, depending on culture and tradition, but for the purposes of our discussion, we need to examine the Christian position, as defined by the Holy Scriptures. The first mention is when the first woman appears:

Then the LORD God made a woman from the rib he had taken out of the man, and he brought her to the man. The man said, "This is now bone of my bones and flesh of my flesh; she shall be called 'woman,' for she was taken out of man." That is why a man leaves his father and mother and is united to his wife, and they become one flesh. (Genesis 2:23-24).

After the Fall this one flesh, this husband and wife, were reprimanded by God. The woman would suffer pain in childbirth and be subject to the man, who would now toil to receive food from the ground. The man, Adam, named his wife Eve, the mother of all the living. A straightforward reading of this story tells us that a key feature of this entity "husband and wife" , one flesh, is the offspring that will flow from this relationship.

Crucially, the underlying issue here is about how we read from the Bible. Firstly, we must always remember that this is God's word – from His perspective rather than ours – and secondly, we should be more concerned with *function* over form. In short, this means that everything in the Bible is put there for a function or purpose and we must always ask ourselves, what is God's purpose for putting it there? So, what is God's purpose for this *one flesh?* Is it primarily about the expression of love between partners? Is it purely about mutual sexual pleasure? Actually, the Bible is silent on this, but it speaks consistently of one purpose: *the production of offspring.* This is God's viewpoint, as featured in the Bible. We are aware that other expressions of one flesh, or marriage, in other cultures, may see things in a different way but the Bible insists that this is His model for propagating the species.

This may seem narrow and judgmental to "modern thinkers" (unfortunately including many Christians) as they try to shake off the old Biblical definitions to justify sexually-driven fashions. We must insist that the Bible is our authority, interpreted correctly as God's instructive wisdom to us. Scripture is not a means of rubber-stamping our own ideas, even some of our Church traditions. Christian marriage is sacred because of the mystery that is wrapped around it. If we seek to redefine this, we are meddling where we shouldn't and God is not to be mocked. We don't make the rules, He does. However unloving it may seem from our limited human perspective, Christian marriage must reflect His Holiness. God has proved His love for humanity and owes us no explanations.

The Scottish Episcopal Church leadership is treading on dangerous ground with serious implications not just for themselves, but also for the wider Anglican denomination. They would do well to heed this warning:

But, dear friends, remember what the apostles of our Lord Jesus Christ foretold. They said to you, "In the last times there will be scoffers who will follow their own ungodly desires." These are the people who divide you, who

follow mere natural instincts and do not have the Spirit.
(Jude 1:17-19).

Rebellion brings division, not true unity. And this is why, from our perspective, *God hates adultery.* It no longer brings a penalty of stoning to death (though it does in some expressions of Islam) but Jesus frowned on it.

You have heard that it was said, 'You shall not commit adultery.' But I tell you that anyone who looks at a woman lustfully has already committed adultery with her in his heart. (Matthew 5:27-28).

As with murder, he dwells on the inner promptings even before they manifest outwardly and 'do the deed'. He was merciful with the woman caught in adultery (John 7:53 and onwards) and certainly rescued her from a stoning, but she was told to sin no more! Mercy triumphed over judgement, from the mouth of our Messiah.

Interestingly the hypocrisy of her accusers is wonderfully reflected in our current society. When John Major was Prime Minister, he initiated a back to basics campaign in October 1993, a return to old-fashioned family values. This was swiftly followed by a string of disclosures of naughtiness among Conservative MPs, from sexual deviancy to fiddling expenses. Then, of course, Major himself was later found out, having conducted a steamy affair with fellow MP, Edwina Currie over a period of four years, between 1984 and 1988. It is plain to see that there really are no role models left apart from Jesus himself. Adultery is not judged any more as a serious crime against society, just a squabble between affected parties. God is no longer in the equation in our post-Christian society.

The Sinner's Charter would have the following entry:

Be discreet in your relationships, so that as few people as possible would be affected by your actions. Of course, society has no right to judge on these personal issues.

To have what's not yours

"You shall not steal." (Exodus 20:15).

A simple command. Perhaps a degree of stating the obvious, *surely the essence of civilised behaviour is to be content with what you have and, if not, work hard to attain what you don't have?* Who said we're civilised, anyway? There are a whole variety of ways we can break this particular commandment. We can be direct and obvious and rob a bank, mug old biddies in the street or raid our kids' piggy banks. Or we can borrow pencils from work (minor perks) or fiddle our expenses in the great tradition set by some of our (right dishonourable) politicians (major perks). Or we can examine the original context.

The Hebrew word here, *ganav*, is singular, implying the stealing of a single object. Elsewhere, in Leviticus 19:11, we also see *you shall not steal*, but, in this case, the word, *ganavu*, is plural, implying the stealing of many things. The rabbis have much to say about this, particularly the influential Rashi. He suggests that the Leviticus verse conveys the traditional view of the commandment, in the sense of stealing money or property, but that the verse etched onto a stone tablet by the Finger of God has a *very different meaning*.

Rashi and other rabbis urge us to look at the context, at the preceding commandments, dealing with murder and adultery, each punishable by death. They insist that the "stealing" being referred to here is the type of stealing that is also punishable by death. A clue is in Exodus 21:16:

Anyone who kidnaps someone is to be put to death, whether the victim has been sold or is still in the kidnapper's possession.

The word here for kidnap is, again, *ganav,* the same word as in the Eighth Commandment. Food for thought, but, as we find with rabbis, not everyone agrees and the consensus is that, although kidnapping may have been the primary context, ordinary acts of stealing, burglary and general thievery are also implied. Because of the vagueness of the Hebrew language (to say nothing of the lack of vowels or punctuations in the original script), the *Midrash* goes further to suggest that the use of the singular and plural forms of the word is a warning against both stealing as a solo act and stealing in the company of others. And, because of this laxity, coupled with some fertile rabbinic minds, other possibilities also spring forth.

• Being discourteous can be seen as stealing. If you greet someone and that greeting is not acknowledged by the other person, then they are deemed a robber for depriving you of the courteous response you deserved! If this was a capital offense then Twitter, that dreadful cradle of bad behaviour, would certainly be the modern equivalent of the 'killing fields'!

• The rabbis even anticipated copyright crime, the bane of writers such as wot I am. The presenting of someone else's ideas as one's own is stealing however you may look at it.

• You don't just have to be the robber to be guilty. Receiving stolen goods is just an incentive to robbers to carry on robbing and the Talmud tells us that accomplices of a thief are as bad as the thief himself.

- We will finish with a strange one, the stealing of someone's feelings by making them feel sorry for us in situations when we don't deserve it. Shades of the fake contrition we see from celebrities who have fallen from their perch and are advised by their PR experts to *show an appropriate amount of sorrow.*

But there is a form of stealing that is very much in line with rabbinic thinking. It doesn't take much thought to widen the act of kidnapping to include slavery and its modern equivalent, *people trafficking.* In fact, when we really consider the implications it is not too hard to be in agreement that the main thrust of the Eighth Commandment is to show *God's abhorrence of the stealing of flesh and blood rather than inanimate objects.*

We start our investigation by posing the uncomfortable question that *isn't the Bible OK with slavery?* It seems to accept it as a norm, a part of the culture of the day:

If any of your people—Hebrew men or women—sell themselves to you and serve you six years, in the seventh year you must let them go free. And when you release them, do not send them away empty-handed. Supply them liberally from your flock, your threshing floor and your winepress. Give to them as the LORD your God has blessed you. Remember that you were slaves in Egypt and the LORD your God redeemed you. That is why I give you this command today. (Deuteronomy 15:12-15).

And masters, treat your slaves in the same way. Do not threaten them, since you know that he who is both their Master and yours is in heaven, and there is no favoritism with him. (Ephesians 6:9).

Slavery in those days was a consequence of war or economic downturns, rather than a proactive activity.

Conquered people tended to be enslaved and destitute people often sold themselves into slavery. Of course, there are grey areas and it wasn't exactly a blueprint for a fair society, but we must remember that People of God have always been 'strangers in a strange land' rather than architects of society. What the Bible does talk about, as we saw in the above passages, is how slaves were treated.

This is a far cry from the awful history of the enslavement of populations on racial grounds and for economic gain, whether it was the third of the population of Western Africa enslaved and deported, or the Arab slave trade in Eastern Africa, or the Aztecs and Incas of Central America, or the hundreds of thousands of Christian boys seized by the Ottoman Turks in order to help run their Empire. This still hasn't gone away in our modern 'progressive' times, slavery is very much alive and kicking. *Human trafficking* is a scourge of our times. Here is the Wikipedia description:

> Human trafficking is the trade of humans for the purpose of forced labour, sexual slavery, or commercial sexual exploitation for the trafficker or others. This may encompass providing a spouse in the context of forced marriage, or the extraction of organs or tissues, including for surrogacy and ova removal. Human trafficking can occur within a country or trans-nationally. Human trafficking is a crime against the person because of the violation of the victim's rights of movement through coercion and because of their commercial exploitation. Human trafficking is the trade in people, especially women and children, and does not necessarily involve the movement of the person from one place to another.

This is now a huge multi-national enterprise with huge profits for the perpetrators. In 2014 it was estimated that forced labour alone accounted for around $150 billion in profits! In 2019 it was even discovered that some of the UK's best-known supermarkets had been selling goods produced by unpaid slave labour in the West Midlands, comprising of vulnerable people trafficked over here from Poland.

"You shall not steal." The implications here are vastly underestimated and largely ignored. Also, as we saw with the previous two Commandments, there is said to be an equivalence between this Eighth Commandment and the *Third* Commandment, taking the Name of God in vain. Evidence is (rather loosely) presented in the form of Hosea 4:2:

There is only cursing, lying and murder, stealing and adultery; they break all bounds, and bloodshed follows bloodshed.

So, what about today. How do our modern-day equivalents to those Rabbis interpret this simple verse of Scripture?

"You shall not steal."

There is, of course, an aspect of stealing unique to our modern culture. It is called *identity theft* and, as it is a form of kidnapping, albeit without much schlepping about, to many it should be a capital offence! It is an attack on what is perhaps the dearest commodity for the liberal middle-classes (who are adequately endowed with the *real* necessary commodities for living), one's *identity*. It is defined as *the deliberate use of someone else's identity, usually as a method to gain a financial advantage or obtain credit and other benefits in the other person's name, and perhaps to the other person's disadvantage or loss. The person whose identity has been assumed may suffer adverse consequences, especially if they are held responsible for the perpetrator's actions.*

It's a kidnapping of everything about the person apart from the person himself, so at least blood isn't spilled.

There are around 100,000 victims of identity theft in the UK annually and it makes up around a half of all frauds. It's brought about a meteoric rise in sales of paper shredders and has ensured that even simple commercial phone transactions can be a nightmare, as either party can't always be sure they are speaking to whom they are meant to be speaking. Identity theft also has a sinister side, when we consider some spiritual manifestations of it, particularly in some parts of the Church. It is surely the biggest irony of history that the most reviled and hated people in history are the most prone to *spiritual* identity theft. Why anyone would want to be a Jew beats me, but many falsely claim to be so, adding a double whammy in some instances by declaring that many current Jews are imposters, despite tracing their ancestry and origins to the horrors of the pogroms and Holocaust. Here are a few examples:

There's a group founded over a hundred years ago in the USA, comprising black people who insist they are the *real* Jewish people. They call themselves *Black African Hebrew Israelites* or various permutations of the same and one of their videos, *Hebrews to Negroes*, has over a half a million views. They tend to believe that the Biblical heroes, from Abraham to Jesus were all people of colour and that a large proportion of Jews are imposters, being descended from an Asian tribe of Gentiles called the *Khazars* in the Middle Ages (who admittedly did convert en masse to Judaism possibly due to their love of chicken soup). This, of course, is nonsense and has been refuted both by reputable historians and DNA evidence. This persistent *meme* crops up again and again though to underpin anti-Semitic theories, with a chief objective to invalidate any historical links that Jews may have to the Land of Israel.

British Israelism follows faulty historical and agenda-ridden theories, with the "ten Lost Tribes of Israel" morphing into tea-drinking, empire-building Englishmen! Then there are the door-knockers/commuter-muggers known as Jehovah Witnesses, who claim they are God's 'chosen people', or at least 144,000 of their most elite followers. This number is taken from Revelation 7, in reference to those sealed from the tribes of Israel. It is interesting that JWs are very literalist when interpreting Revelation except when this disrupts their theology, so, instead prefer to *steal the identity* of these Israelites for themselves! Then we have the *Supercessionists*, following 'replacement theology' to also steal the 'spiritual' identity and destiny of the Jewish people and, sadly, at the other end of the spectrum, some Gentiles in the Hebrew Roots movement intent on stealing their physical identity, even to the extent of dressing up in Jewish ritual clothing, speaking pidgin Yiddish, renaming themselves with Hebrew names and, in extreme cases, even getting circumcised!

What on earth is all this about? What is their motive? Is it just an innate anti-Semitism compelling them to act in this way? Or is it fulfilling some sort of need, perhaps a dissatisfaction with their current status and identity? Either way it is a straight contradiction of some key Scriptures:

For I am not ashamed of the gospel, because it is the

power of God that brings salvation to everyone who believes: first to the Jew, then to the Gentile (Romans 1:16).

... but glory, honour and peace for everyone who does good: first for the Jew, then for the Gentile. (Romans 2:10).

There are Jews and there are Gentiles. There aren't any *Jewtiles* or *Genews* or any other mixture, it is black and white, or should I say, *yiddische* and *goyische!*

One thing is clear. Any whiff of real anti-Semitic persecution and those folk will be scuttling under the nearest carpet faster than you can say 'Adolph Eichmann'. Fair weather Jews they may be but, let's not forget that *this is stealing*, no question, and these people are one day going to be answerable to a Higher Power to explain their actions.

Finally, let's get into the nitty gritty because, whereas the *form* of stealing is a straightforward shift of ownership from the legal owner to an illegal owner, whether it is goods, people or identity, it's always the *function* that is the most revealing. We start off with a Biblical reality:

For who makes you different from anyone else? What do you have that you did not receive? And if you did receive it, why do you boast as though you did not? (1 Corinthians 4:7).

The earth is the LORD's, and everything in it, the world, and all who live in it; (Psalm 24:1)

... for every animal of the forest is mine, and the cattle on a thousand hills. (Psalm 50:10).

All that we have comes from God, whatever the World tells us. Whether it is money, good looks, family, or life itself, all has a single origin. This means that if we acquire anything unlawfully, outside the functioning of the laws of barter or commerce, then we are not stealing from a person ... but from God Himself. And the consequences will ultimately be from God Himself! That is the function that lies at the heart of stealing, *an offence against God*. Unfortunately, this will not be reflected in the Sinner's Charter, which firmly takes a human rather than a Divine perspective:

Stealing of possessions is an offence against society and should be duly punished. The stealing of human beings is also wrong and ought to be punished if possible.

To have a loose grip on reality

"You shall not give false testimony against your neighbour." (Exodus 20:16).

The apostle Paul was languishing in Herod's Palace in Caesarea, having been sent there by a Roman commander, as a result of accusations by the Jewish authorities in Jerusalem. He was going to have his case heard by Felix, the Governor. But, first, the Jews presented their case:

"We have found this man to be a troublemaker, stirring up riots among the Jews all over the world. He is a ringleader of the Nazarene sect and even tried to desecrate the temple; so we seized him. By examining him yourself you will be able to learn the truth about all these charges we are bringing against him." (Acts 24:5-8).

This, of course, was complete nonsense. This was false testimony. Today we would call this *Fake News*. Paul responded to these claims:

"You can easily verify that no more than twelve days ago I went up to Jerusalem to worship. My accusers did not find me arguing with anyone at the temple, or stirring up a crowd in the synagogues or anywhere else in the city. And they cannot prove to you the charges they are now making against me … After an absence of several years, I came to Jerusalem to bring my people gifts for the poor and to present offerings. I was ceremonially clean when they found me in the temple courts doing this. There was no crowd with me, nor was I involved in any disturbance." (Acts 24:11-13;17-18).

People have always been quite willing to lie to get their own way. Cain set the tone for this:

"Then the LORD said to Cain, 'Where is your brother Abel?' 'I don't know,' he replied. 'Am I my brother's keeper?'" (Genesis 4:9).

Fake News may have received notoriety in the Trump era, but it has been simmering on the back burner for many years. The Jewish people have been at the receiving end of it ever since Pharaoh panicked his people into thinking that the Hebrews were a fifth column ready to overthrow the kingdom. Here is an excerpt from *Outcast Nation:*

... And we're not talking of just one alleged Jewish conspiracy; there's a whole swathe of them. Whispers are heard of the Protocols of the Elders of Zion. Zionism is seen as a front for world domination, with the Israeli secret service (Mossad) pulling the strings. Then there are the Illuminati, the Freemasons, the United Nations, the New World Order, the Communists, the International Monetary Fund (IMF), the World Bank and the World's press. Apparently, all have been sucked into the Jewish web! Jews have been put forward as the primary cause of most of the major problems that have weakened European society in the past 200 years such as: World War I, World War II, communism, socialism, liberalism, capitalism, mass immigration, forced integration, racial preference laws, and media bias. Such busy bees, we've been!

The Protocols of the Elders of Zion is probably the most well-known weapon in the armoury of anti-Jewish conspiracy nuts. It is also a complete forgery, but why should the truth get in the way of a good yarn? It is claimed to be the minutes of a meeting of Jewish leaders at the first Zionist congress in Basel, Switzerland in 1897 (or, as some say, a graveyard in Prague), when the Jews were hatching an audacious plot to take over the World!

What it actually was is not that easy to follow. It seems to be based on a pamphlet written at the turn of the 20th Century by a Russian forger as a means to discredit reforms in that country and bolster the influence of the Czar. This forger took material from a satire on Napoleon III by Maurice Joly and from a novel by Hermann Goedesche, a 19th Century German anti-Semite. The final form of the Protocols first appeared in Russia in around 1905, becoming a best seller by 1920 and promoted in the USA by none other than Henry Ford, who when he wasn't building cars was ranting and raving about Jews. It was first exposed as a forgery by Philip Graves of The Times in 1921, not before one Adolph Hitler had a chance to read it and believe it.

Most of the other so-called Jewish conspiracies are simply variations on the theme or strategies to achieve World domination over the last few hundred years. Let's summarise a few of them:

- in 1775 Jews finance the American Revolution.

- in 1933 Jews conspired against the Germans and caused World War II.

- in 1990 Jews conspired against the Iraqis and caused the Gulf War.

- in 1999 Jews conspired to incite the bombing of Serbs in Serbia (The Serbian Defence League website, is subtitled documenting Zionist genocides on Serbs.)

- in 2001 Jews were the real instigators of 9-11.

- Jews have instigated, supported and financed World War I, the Cold War, the Korean War, the Vietnam War as part of a perpetual Jewish war against the rest of the world.

- Jews control the United States government through an organization known as ZOG (Zionist Occupation Government.)

Finally, the most repulsive, sinister and intellectually corrupt claim of all; the one that affirms that the Holocaust never happened, despite thousands of Jewish (and Gentile) eye witnesses, Nazi documents, newsreels and other photographic evidence. They suggest that the Holocaust was a Jewish conspiracy, a lie simply to engender sympathy from the World for the Jewish plight and yearning for a homeland of their own. One such Holocaust-denier, David Irving, sued an American academic, Deborah Lipstadt, in 2002 for claiming that he is a 'Hitler partisan' who twists history to cast the German dictator in a better light. He lost his case and his house and was declared bankrupt ...

So we can see that *Fake News* is far more sinister than the mischievous mis-information we encounter today revolving around the lives of celebrities, politicians and basically anyone in the public eye.

Of course, Fake News cuts no ice with God, Who sees everything and acts accordingly. But does this commandment *actually mean what it says on the tin?* What is the literal reading of the Hebrew words?

Although we translate the passage as *no false testimony,* the more literal translation is *no answering or repeating.* It focuses not just at the point of embarkation of the gossip grapevine, but at all points thereafter! It is an injunction against *hearsay,* it is the repeating of the story that is frowned upon. The thinking is that the subject of the gossip may actually be true, but, unless you were an actual primary witness, you are indulging in hearsay. So, attempting to unpack the scope of this commandment, giving false testimony or propagating Fake News is bad enough, but also is the repeating of the testimony of others, or gossiping is also bad. So, no lying and no gossiping ... even if *I had it on the best authority ...*

If the broader interpretation is correct, then most of our News media has been rendered unacceptable. When reporting on any event, only verifiable eye-witness accounts can be used, all opinion and commentary are to be discounted. It's not just a case of whether the news is fake or real, it's also a matter of whether there are witnesses to it. Here's an example of the importance of such a principal:

In April 2002 the media was in a frenzy about the "Jenin Massacre" in Israel, with news reports from such as the BBC and the *Guardian,* presenting such headlines as *'Jenin massacre evidence growing'* and clear reporting of a massacre by Israeli forces. A month later, to their credit, the *Guardian* had this to say:

> "Despite flimsy evidence British papers jumped the gun to apportion blame when a West Bank refugee camp was attacked, says Sharon Sadeh. As a result, the reputation of the press has been damaged ... The battle of Jenin was indisputably

fierce and bloody. But while the British papers, almost unanimously, presented it from the outset as a "massacre" or at least as an intentional "war crime" of the worst kind, the US and Israeli papers - Ha'aretz included - were far more reserved and cautious, saying that there was no evidence to back such claims. The left-liberal press in Britain thought differently. The Independent, the Guardian and the Times, in particular, were quick to denounce Israel and made sensational accusations based on thin evidence, fitting a widely held stereotype of a defiant, brutal and don't-give-a-damn Israel."

Apparently one of the drivers for the original emotive reporting by the *Times, Telegraph* and *Guardian*, was the obviously flawed testimony of a single individual, Kamal Anis, who claimed to witness Israeli war crimes. The reporters, in a clear dereliction of the independence required in war journalism, heard and believed what they wanted to hear and believe. The *Guardian* article continues:

"Selective use of details or information and occasional reliance on unsubstantiated accounts inflict considerable damage on the reputation of the entire British press, and more importantly, do a disservice to its readers. The US media, especially the press, were wilfully oblivious, prior to the September 11 attacks, to the issues which might have captured more accurately and profoundly the realities regarding the Middle East and the Muslim world, and the appropriate way of approaching and handling them. Are the British media in a similar state of self-denial?"

In this case the news story came from a single witness, who was lying through his teeth. The British press fed from this, added their own colour to the story and ended up with Fake News. But it also shows us a sad reality regarding the information that is fed to us through the numerous media channels available. Everything is 'editorialised' or *spun*, in accordance with the politics, religion, philosophy or lifestyle of the people channelling the information. It seems that most of us are too deadened to the truth to care and, in fact, most of us would seek out our news sources from those whose politics / religion / philosophy / lifestyle we agree with. Where does the absolute truth fit in here? Well, except in clear cut cases where facts are impervious to spin, such as natural disasters, the absolute truth will only be found in sources *that actually believe in the absolute truth*. I rest my case here.

"You shall not give false testimony."

As we saw with the previous three Commandments, there is said to be an equivalence between this Ninth Commandment and the *Fourth* Commandment, regarding the keeping of the *Sabbath*. Here is the thinking. The Sabbath is a day when Israel testifies that God created the Earth, so whoever desecrates the Sabbath denies the truth of this testimony and bears false witness to the Works of God. If this is so, then the Church has a lot to answer for both by moving the Sabbath to a Sunday and also by denying the literal six days of Creation. Can it be bearing a false witness? A serious statement has been made here, one that affects everyone who identifies with the Church.

Here is how the Sinner's Charter could interpret this ninth Commandment:

Fake News is indeed the scourge of our times but sometimes we need to follow the narrative and take into account different interpretations of an event. Nothing is ever black and white, truth is an ever-moving target, it is not an absolute.

To cast greedy eyes around and about

"You shall not covet your neighbour's house. You shall not covet your neighbor's wife, or his male or female servant, his ox or donkey, or anything that belongs to your neighbour." (Exodus 20:17).

In terms of the lifeblood of our economy, the phenomenon of gambling ranks as one of the major players. These days it is sanitised and made respectable. You'd be hard-pressed to find a football team not sponsored by an on-line betting company these days. To my way of thinking *you don't get 'owt for nowt*. Everyone who bets is expecting (foolishly) to get unearned cash and this money has to come from somewhere? Other foolish gamblers! This is state-sponsored covetousness. Our eyes seem to be pre-programmed to be cast around and about, at the good fortunes of others, or even guided by the thought that, *I want what he's got, even if I don't really need it. I just don't like it that he has it and I don't!*

So, we have a flow of money fuelled by rampant coveting, with a nice little dividend creamed off the top by the facilitators. Those "sophisticated" gamblers, the bankers and stock market dabblers are no different, they are also filling (or emptying) their pockets with unearned money. But there's a difference here, where greedy gamblers can very easily bring down companies, banks, even countries, with ordinary people suffering. Livelihoods are stolen through the greed of others. Unfortunately, there's no law against these activities, except in cases of insider trading, so our general discontent with what the Lord has given us in life is very much a key driver in society.

We are all consumers, encouraged by the advertisers and marketeers to feed the system, despite the inequality at the heart of it. To re-iterate what we said about stealing in an earlier chapter: All that we have comes from God, whatever the World tells us. Whether it is money, good looks, family, or life itself, all has a single origin. This means that if we acquire anything unlawfully, outside the functioning of the laws of barter or commerce, then we are not stealing from a person ... but from God Himself. And the consequences will ultimately be from God Himself! That is the function that lies at the heart of stealing, *an offence against God.* Although coveting doesn't always lead to stealing, it is certainly a great encouragement to *go out and get what you don't have.*

Keep your life free from love of money, and be content with what you have, for he has said, "I will never leave you nor forsake you." (Hebrews 13:5).

Wealth gained hastily will dwindle, but whoever gathers little by little will increase it. (Proverbs 13:11).

It is time now to dig into the Hebrew behind the "commandment":

"You shall not covet your neighbour's house. You shall not covet your neighbour's wife, or his male or female servant, his ox or donkey, or anything that belongs to your neighbour."

The Hebrew word here, *chamad,* indeed takes the general meaning of "covet", but what about the equivalent word in the parallel passage in Deuteronomy?

"You shall not covet your neighbour's wife. You shall not

set your desire on your neighbor's house or land, his male or female servant, his ox or donkey, or anything that belongs to your neighbor." (Deuteronomy 5:21).

Two Hebrew words are used here, *chamad* and *avah*. Although both can mean "covet", the second word conveys another emotion, *desire*. The Rabbis suggest that desire can lead to coveting, which could then lead to stealing: *They covet fields and seize them, and houses, and take them.* (Micah 2:2). And this could go even further to be prepared to kill in order to acquire that which you covet. Here's a story that is worth recounting:

Some time later there was an incident involving a vineyard belonging to Naboth the Jezreelite. The vineyard was in Jezreel, close to the palace of Ahab king of Samaria. Ahab said to Naboth, "Let me have your vineyard to use for a vegetable garden, since it is close to my palace. In exchange I will give you a better vineyard or, if you prefer, I will pay you whatever it is worth." But Naboth replied, "The LORD forbid that I should give you the inheritance of my ancestors." So Ahab went home, sullen and angry because Naboth the Jezreelite had said, "I will not give you the inheritance of my ancestors." He lay on his bed sulking and refused to eat. His wife Jezebel came in and asked him, "Why are you so sullen? Why won't you eat?" He answered her, "Because I said to Naboth the Jezreelite, 'Sell me your vineyard; or if you prefer, I will give you another vineyard in its place.' But he said, 'I will not give you my vineyard.'" Jezebel his wife said, "Is this how you act as king over Israel? Get up and eat! Cheer up. I'll get you the vineyard of Naboth the Jezreelite."

So she wrote letters in Ahab's name, placed his seal on them, and sent them to the elders and nobles who lived in

*Naboth's city with him. In those letters she wrote:
"Proclaim a day of fasting and seat Naboth in
prominent place among the people. But seat two
scoundrels opposite him and have them bring charges that
he has cursed both God and the king. Then take him out
and stone him to death." So the elders and nobles who
lived in Naboth's city did as Jezebel directed in the letters
she had written to them. They proclaimed a fast and
seated Naboth in a prominent place among the people.
Then two scoundrels came and sat opposite him and
brought charges against Naboth before the people, saying,
"Naboth has cursed both God and the king." So they took
him outside the city and stoned him to death. Then they
sent word to Jezebel: "Naboth has been stoned to death."
As soon as Jezebel heard that Naboth had been stoned to
death, she said to Ahab, "Get up and take possession of the
vineyard of Naboth the Jezreelite that he refused to sell
you. He is no longer alive, but dead." When Ahab heard
that Naboth was dead, he got up and went down to take
possession of Naboth's vineyard.* (1 Kings 21:1-16).

You have to give it to the evil Jezebel, there are not too
many people that can break five separate commandments
to get their own way (the third, sixth, eighth, ninth and
tenth!). Her reputation is well earned!

So, it's very much a slippery pole! How do we train
ourselves away from our propensity to covet, bearing in
mind that it's a basic human nature to desire attractive
things, both animate and inanimate? The rabbis suggest
that it is a matter of perspective and illustrate it with the
parable of the poor peasant who casts his eyes, for the first
time, on the beautiful but unattainable princess. Way out
of his class, on a totally different orbit. Her status is so out
of reach that he has an in-built acceptance that he has no
hope in coveting her hand in marriage, so the situation

does not trouble him. We should think in the same way. We should accept that all we acquire is a direct gift from God, Who determines all of our needs and supplies them accordingly. No-one can interfere with this Divine plan, neither should we interfere with the needs of others, who are also partakers of this plan. So coveting is not an option. Here's how we should think, *God is the Master of my fate, not I and if I deserve to own something then He will provide it and not withhold it from me. But if we are not destined to acquire something, then all your pains or efforts to do so will come to naught, so why bother striving?*

A noble thought, but the reality is illustrated in the following lines from a song produced by an American Christian hip-hop group:

We worship how we feel, we don't worship who we should. Yeah we got it bad, and if God calls it bad we call it good. We covet what others have, grab whatever we can, whatever we want, we think it belongs in the palm of our hands, going along with a song and a dance. Worshipping idols to fulfil our entitlement issues. (An excerpt from 'Entitlement' by Beautiful Eulogy).

Entitlement. Now, there's a word for today. It is tied up with the idea of our rights, as if we really have any in the great (Divine) scheme of things. It is a product of the #AllAboutMe culture that we live in, encouraged, or rather, *driven*, by the relentless trajectory of those who call themselves 'progressives', with an unholy rush to jettison our Judeo-Christian foundations – which of course include the "Ten Commandments" – towards a goal disguised as a new world of tolerant inclusion but which, in fact, is a twisted utopia of aimlessness and lawlessness. Most don't realise this as they are just *going with the flow,* because they are told that it is the right thing and are blinded to what lays ahead. One thing is certain - it will bear no likeness to what has been left behind. The Sinner's Charter will be a recipe for everyone to do what they want, rather than the "original" model that was a guide for righteous living. The Sinner's Charter is a perfect companion to those who live by the rule of entitlement.

Entitlement suggests that you drive a bigger car than your cousin Mitchell, who seems to have everything else in life. Let's hope we can keep making those repayments.

Entitlement considers it unfair that the scruffy bloke next door has such an attractive wife. It should be easy to steal her virtue and what fun it will be in the chase.

Entitlement compels you to add a few extra items on that insurance claim. It's not really cheating, as the insurance companies are mega rich and, after all, it will help pay towards that Jamaican holiday you've always craved.

The possessions we have, whether acquired at God's pleasure or as a result of coveting, are *forms*, just objects. They are unimportant in the great scheme of things. What is important though is how you acquired them, the *function*. If you can say that, in good conscience, that your "stuff" is how it should be, then blessings are assured. But bear in mind that this covers all aspects of your life, including your money and even your relationships. Everything belongs to God.

"You shall not covet ...."

As we saw with the previous four commandments, there is said to be an equivalence between this final commandment and the *Fifth* Commandment, concerning honouring one's parents. To be honest, the rabbis haven't presented a compelling case for this, which doesn't mean there isn't one, it's just that they haven't found it yet! One suggests that someone who covets will bear children who will fail to honour him. Another suggests that one who covets another's property is not fulfilling their duty with their own property, so how are they expected to support their parents in their old age (?). Yet another suggests that one who covets another man's wife will bring spiritual complications to his own marriage and will give birth to children who will bring him misery! The jury is still out ...

One final thought though. Coveting was, in fact, the first sin and so, arguably, the root of all evil, the sin that brought about The Fall.

When the woman saw that the fruit of the tree was good for food and pleasing to the eye, and also desirable for gaining wisdom, she took some and ate it. She also gave some to her husband, who was with her, and he ate it. (Genesis 3:6).

We can add to this the stories of Cain (coveted Abel's favour with God), Korah (ditto with Moses), also Balaam, Doeg, Achitophel, Gehazi, Absalom, Adonijah, Uzziah and Haman. Now there's a little Bible study for you, if you take the challenge.

Here is how the Sinner's Charter could interpret this final Commandment:

There is nothing wrong with having the ambition to strive to legally acquire what you don't have. There is nothing wrong with fulfilling your desires.

PART TWO
The Journey

Early delving and spinning

12

Why can't we just leave things alone? We humans have added our particular spin on timeless truths since Adam delved and Eve span (to quote out of context!) Such was to be the journey of the "Ten Commandments", once Christians got their hands on it. Nothing much was heard for the first three centuries until Augustine of Hippo appeared on the scene in the 4th Century, producing a series of sermons on the subject, rather than detailed expositions. It just wasn't a subject that motivated Christian thinkers and writers, probably because it wasn't *a salvation issue*. We have to wait until the 14th Century for the next significant development, the writings of the Greek Orthodox Gregory of Palamas, the Bishop of Thessalonica. As with other mystical thinkers of his tradition, he was looking to add a Christian slant to the "Commandments", making them relevant for his generation. So, he took the "Ten Commandments" and ...

First of all, he altered God's "calling card", from the Jewish, *"I am the Lord your God who brought you out from Egypt ..."* to the Gentile Christian *"The Lord God is one, known in Father and in Son and in Holy Spirit ..."*. Then, in the same vein, he asserted the prohibition against idolatry by referring to the Nicene Creed, but didn't totally follow the spirit of the Second Commandment by not totally condemning the use of images and icons in the Church. He modifies the Third Commandment, merging it with the Ninth Commandment and declaring that it is to do with perjury and false witness, rather than blasphemy. Already the "Ten Commandments" are being redefined as *the response of man, rather than reflecting the heart of God*. This is reinforced by his take on the Fourth Commandment, where the Biblical Sabbath has already given way to the "Lord's Day", Saturday becomes Sunday. Honouring one's parents now has conditions attached, only honour them if they draw you closer to God, *otherwise flee from them*. On the other hand, you are always exhorted to honour your *spiritual* father, the priest! He says little about adultery because holy men are surely above such things, even marriage is frowned upon here, *the refuge of the weak* (without whom, of course, the human race would have died out!). To murder is to swap ownership from Christ to Satan, he is quite black and white here, no grey areas. Stealing is shown as an alternative to the doing of charitable acts, which are to be encouraged. Bearing false witness is presented as a warning against slandering another and coveting is presented as the very root of sin.

All in all, Gregory's list is primarily for the clergy, the rest perhaps were considered of little consequence. It is worth now looking at the writings of a layman, a Richard Rolle, an English hermit from the 14th Century. Here's what he had to say: Regarding idolatry, although magic charms and sorcery are forbidden, crucifixes and statues of saints are to be revered. God's name was still not allowed to be taken in vain and there are three ways one could sin through swearing in God's name; swearing against what you actually believe in, swearing by Christ's wounds or blood and not carrying out that which you have sworn to do. The Sabbath commandment is read as Sunday observance, when one must abandon all wicked behaviour. Honouring parents is maintained, both physically and spiritually. Murder is prohibited, but an addition is *spiritual* murder, those who refuse to feed the poor, who slander others and who mislead the innocent. He is also firm on adultery and theft, the latter including a whole plethora of laws protecting the property of the King and the ruling classes. False witness is frowned upon and the worst kind of lying – mortal sins – are when people are harmed spiritually or physically. Coveting is also dealt with, bound by the golden rule of not inflicting on someone that which you wouldn't want inflicted on yourself.

So Gregory's list was in the Catholic tradition of including elements of the Nicene creed and was particularly relevant to those in the clergy, whereas Rolle's was more earthy and general, centred more on conduct between people, rather than God's requirements. Now we stay in England, but travel back in time to the person who is most associated with creating a foundation of lawfulness, based on Christian principles (when he wasn't burning cakes).

Alfred the Great lived in the 9th Century and attempted to build up a civil code of conduct based on the Ten Commandments. Winston Churchill, when considering Alfred's life, stated that here "we are witnessing the birth of a Nation". His law code began with an introduction containing a translation of the Ten Commandments into English. These were to be the basis of the law for a Christian nation if it wished to be blessed by God and Christian principles formed his concept of justice as he chose the laws which were to form the basis of the legal system. This was the beginning of our English legal system, the "Common Law" that was going to hold sway centuries later. Here's his basic list (with the Second Commandment strangely relegated to the bottom of the list and the Sabbath not mentioned by name!):

1) "Do not love other strange gods before Me!"

2) "Do not call out My Name in idleness! For you are not guiltless with Me, if you call out My Name in idleness."

3) "Mind that you hallow the rest-day! You must work six days; but on the seventh you must rest! For in six days Christ made Heavens and Earth, the seas, and all the shapen things in them; but He rested on the seventh day. Therefore, the Lord hallowed it."

4) "Honour your father and your mother whom the Lord gave you – so that you may live longer on Earth!"

5) "Do not slay!"

6) "Do not commit adultery!"

7) "Do not steal!"

8) "Do not witness falsely!"

9) "Do not unrighteously desire your neighbour's goods!"

10) "Do not make gold or silver gods for yourself!"

His law code also contains some other verses from Exodus as well as Acts 15:23-29:

With them they sent the following letter: The apostles and elders, your brothers, To the Gentile believers in Antioch, Syria and Cilicia: Greetings. We have heard that some went out from us without our authorization and disturbed you, troubling your minds by what they said. So we all agreed to choose some men and send them to you with our dear friends Barnabas and Paul— men who have risked their lives for the name of our Lord Jesus Christ. Therefore we are sending Judas and Silas to confirm by word of mouth what we are writing. It seemed good to the Holy Spirit and to us not to burden you with anything beyond the following requirements: You are to abstain from food sacrificed to idols, from blood, from the meat of strangled animals and from sexual immorality. You will do well to avoid these things.

These writings from Alfred were his musings on how best to introduce Mosaic law to his English nation, underpinning his thoughts with Scripture in order to place a Divine seal on it. Although he stressed Christ's mercy to all, his emphasis was on the feudal hierarchy that existed in his day and re-interpreted *"love your neighbour as yourself"* (Matthew 22:39–40) as *"love your secular lord as you would love the Lord Christ himself"*. Everyone still had to understand their place in society, with Kings and Lords definitely at the top of the heap. His law code itself was a bit of a random mess, with little logic to tie it all together. Historians suggest that these should be viewed in a symbolic sense – as a manifesto of kingship – rather than as a practical set of laws that could be used.

We move on to medieval times, to Thomas Aquinas, the key Catholic theologian and philosopher of his day and who had much to say about the Ten Commandments, from these two perspectives. In fact, he had more to say on the Law of Moses, mainly because the burning question for theologians at that time was *what do Christians do about the Laws in the Old Testament?* It was a period when, on the one hand, there was an interest in *literal meanings* of Scripture, but on the other hand, the works of Aristotle were becoming popular, bringing ideas and thought-patterns from the world of philosophy. These two concepts brought something new to the table, a desire to investigate logical "reasons" for God's laws. In other words, they were bringing God and His actions, thoughts and motives down to a human level. They wanted to pick Him apart, using their rational minds as a set of tweezers! As a theologian he introduces the Commandments as part of the Christian creed and as part of the process of individual salvation, in reminding ourselves of our sin nature. He offers detailed commentary alongside each Commandment. For instance, alongside the First Commandment he offers suggestions of who these 'other gods' may be and offers five motives of why we should worship the One God only; the dignity of the Creator, His generosity in sharing being, the necessity of renouncing the devil, avoiding slavery to the devil and how to achieve eternal life.

As a philosopher he defers to the rational approach of Aristotle, viewing God as the 'Prime Mover', the First and the Final Cause in the World. His biggest challenge was to square up the Ten Commandments with the teachings of this pagan Greek philosopher. At the outset I must declare that this was a bad thing and that Aquinas did major damage to the Church through his compromising Biblical truths in order to fit in with alien philosophy (more of this in *How the Church Lost the Truth*). So let us move on ...

The Reformation brought new ideas and we start with John Wycliffe, the 'morning star of the Reformation' who came on the scene a century earlier, in the 14th Century. For Wycliffe, to obey the commandments is to honour God duly. He slightly tweaks the list:

1. I am the Lord your God ... (he follows the lead of the Jews here and, also, he implies the prohibition on idol making/worshipping here too)
2. Don't take the Name of the Lord in vain
3. Keep the Sabbath (Sunday!)

4. Honour your parents (also treat your neighbours as you would want to be treated)
5. Do not murder
6. Do not commit adultery (bodily or spiritually)
7. Do not steal
8. No false witness
9. Don't covet your neighbour's house
10. Don't covet your neighbour's wife, ox etc.

Yet, in the period that follows, many versions of the Ten Commandments circulated, up to a dozen of them, many of them inaccurate paraphrases or verses. Here's an example of the First Commandment: *'Thou shalt have, neither night nor day, none other God but the king of bliss'*. And the Tenth Commandment: *'Desire not thy neighbour's wife, though she be fair and white as a swan, and thy wife brown.'* Poetry and political-correctness were evidently not their forte!

A century later, Martin Luther came on the scene, bringing with him the Reformation of the Church. Yet his reading of the Ten Commandments was no real deviation from Catholic understandings, apart from one of them (read on). In other words, he didn't, in the spirit of *Sola Scriptura*, start from scratch with a literal rendition of Exodus 20 and Deuteronomy 5. Nevertheless, they were important to him, they are ways in which we are to "fear and love God". His most interesting adjustments, though, were to the sixth commandment, *thou shalt not commit adultery.*

Remember he was an ex-monk who married a nun, so his view on the chastity of the clergy is not exactly going to be the mainstream Catholic position. He went as far as to declare that celibacy was sinful! This actually brought him in line with the Jewish position, where rabbis are positively encouraged to marry and have large families.

His fellow "revolutionary", John Calvin, made great use of the Ten Commandments in his doctrinal statements (catechisms), sermons and commentaries. In fact, he was to produce the definitive Protestant commentary of the commandments in his day. He also used the commandments to enforce discipline in the "kingdom" he had built in Geneva, with the Spanish "freethinker", Servetus, even burnt at the stake for blasphemy! He was also strong on the keeping of the (Sunday) Sabbath and the commandment against adultery. He looked for ways to reduce 'temptations of the flesh' including advising married couples to restrain any fruity behaviour and banning public dancing.

The Puritans were very hot on the Ten Commandments, parents teaching them religiously to their children, aided by a guide written in 1681 by Joseph Waite. In this he tells them, *"thou shall teach (these words) diligently unto thy children and shalt talk of them when thou sittest in thou house and when thou walkest by the way and when thou liest down and when thou risest up"*. In other words, he covered all bases! He was especially hot on the (Sunday) Sabbath and devoted much of his guide detailing the dos and don'ts for this special day.

A later Puritan, Jonathan Edwards in America in the 18th Century took an approach to the Ten Commandments suggested by the Gospels. He appealed to John 13:34-35 to declare that the rules of Christ now hold sway, the *New Commandment.*

"A new command I give you: Love one another. As I have loved you, so you must love one another. By this everyone will know that you are my disciples, if you love one another."

He was a highly regarded theologian and philosopher and saw the commandments as a stepping stone towards one of the 'unalienable truths' that emerged from that period in American history, *that all men are created equal and have a natural right to life, liberty and the pursuit of happiness.*

Nevertheless, not everyone had such a benevolent attitude towards the Ten Commandments. In the next chapter we will investigate the flip side ...

Later churning and dissembling

13

As society in the West became less Biblically-motivated and more inclined towards man's perceived needs than God's suggestions, the impact of the Ten Commandments as *religious statements* began to dwindle. We enter the age of the modern philosophers.

Thomas Hobbes, in the 16th Century, saw the Commandments as political, to help the rulers to establish peace and keep the population in order. He was the son of an Anglican priest and, despite being the tutor of Charles II, rebelled to a sufficient degree to have his books banned by the Catholic Church and Oxford University. He had no care for the inner life and the salvation of the soul, his view of the Commandments are simply as practical rules that the dutiful citizen was obliged to follow, as interpreted by the King. He had a high view of the King but a pessimistic view of the life of the common man, "poor, solitary, nasty, brutish and short". His philosophy even gave powers to the King to decide the choice of religion for his people, so it is clear that he had little grasp of Biblical faith and the free will of man.

John Locke, in the 17th Century, was the best known of the English philosophers. He was one of the architects of the *Glorious Revolution*, the plot to install William of Orange as Protestant king of England, to keep the Catholics at bay and also one of the brains behind the Constitution of the United States. He was an *empiricist*, who test everything and rely on practice rather than theory. His interpretation of the Ten Commandments was as a set of moral imperatives, his catchphrase would be *do this and live.* The emphasis was not on acts of a born-again believer, but rather conduct brought about through a rational mind. He could see the English Constitution, the legal underpinning of our Nation, as a set of statutes that owe their origin to the Commandments, if not their current form.

In the 18th Century Baron de La Brede et de Montesquieu had both a grand name and grand designs on formulating a moral code for the society in which he lived. His plan was a pragmatic one, to compare various religious and secular codes and decide which would work for the best. Which was the most useful religion for a stable society? He plundered the Ten Commandments without quoting from them and, with input from the Noahic and Essene codes, mixed with the ancient Greek Stoics, formulated a moral code containing fourteen principles, some of them a bit woolly and obscure to our modern ears; to observe justice, to do no ill to anyone, to keep faith, to hate injustice, to command with modesty, to always be truthful, to avoid unlawful gain, to carry that which signals true greatness, to despise pleasure and pain, to be a good citizen, to regard riches as vanity, to labour for the happiness of mankind, to exercise one's duties and to honour the sacred spirit within all. There is, in common with the thinking of the day, little 'God' element in this list.

Immanuel Kant was the great rationalist at that time. Although raised as a Christian, the central principals of *his thoughts* were ... his thoughts. He paid lip service to the Commandments only in the sense of the Gospel summary, *love God above everything and thy neighbour as thyself.* Thomas Jefferson, in the USA around the same time, was a bit more generous but still saw everything, even the

Commandments, through the lens of his own rational mind. He would particularly stress three of them, not to murder, steal or bear false witness but was dismissive of the rest of them.

Later in the 18th Century came Jeremy Bentham, one of the fiercest critics of the Ten Commandments. He was the founder of the Utilitarian Movement, where right actions are judged by their usefulness and consequences. *Do they produce pleasure or pain* was one consideration? *The greatest happiness for the greatest number,* was another. Bentham was unimpressed with the use of the Commandments as a basis of the human laws of England, despite Alfred the Great getting the ball rolling all of those centuries earlier. His was a rejection of God at the outset, rejecting God's laws was just a consequence of this. Hegel, in the same century, was also no friend of God's laws. He created a philosophy of history that viewed the Ten Commandments as a *primitive, tribal and exclusive code of a superstitious Oriental people (the Jews).*

In the 19th Century, Arthur Hugh Clough, a noted poet and assistant to Florence Nightingale, wrote the following satirical poem about the Ten Commandments, *the Latest Decalogue:*

Thou shalt have one God only; who would tax himself to worship two?

God's image nowhere shalt thou see, save haply in the currency:

Swear not at all; since for thy curse thine enemy is not the worse:

At church on Sunday to attend will help to keep the world thy friend:

Honour thy parents; that is, all from whom promotion may befall:

Thou shalt not kill; but needst not strive officiously to keep alive:

Adultery it is not fit or safe, for women, to commit:

Thou shalt not steal; an empty feat, when 'tis so lucrative to cheat:

False witness not to bear be strict; and cautious, ere you contradict.

Thou shalt not covet; but tradition sanctions the keenest competition.

As with all satire, it speaks cuttingly into the cultural climate of the day and this poem served to show up the hypocrisy and lip service to moral issues that prevailed in those times in England.

Also in the 19th Century, the empty-souled Friedrich Nietzsche, the man who declared *God is dead. God remains dead. And we have killed him* carries on this destructive trend. He had a twisted trust that Man would create universal goals to supplant God's laws, which turned out an impossibility as eternal truths have to be viewed objectively and anything that comes out of the mind of flawed man is always going to be subjective, biased and self-serving. This has given us the horrendously evil morality of Marxism and Nazism and countless other dangerous ideas in the 20th Century. Nietzsche also said, *"each one of us should devise his own virtue, his own categorical imperative. A people perishes if it mistakes his own duty for the concept of duty in general"*. In other words, we all decide what is right and what's right for you may not be right for me. The Ten Commandments, with its *absolute truth*, runs counter to this and no wonder Nietzsche hated it and called it an affront to man's freedom to choose.

Our current postmodern society follows on the trend

started by the rationalist philosophers, then further developed by Nietzsche and Marx, providing an environment where objective truth is so undervalued that the Ten Commandments are seen as having no validity at all and have morphed into an upside-down parody, *The Sinners Charter.*

Current fumbling and mumbling   14

As the Ten Commandments entered our world very much through a Jewish context, it is puzzling when we consider how modern Judaism has mostly neglected them, in terms of liturgy, even though they are prominently displayed on synagogue walls. They appear in the annual cycle of weekly *Torah* portions and are recited at the annual feast of *Shavuot*, yet are strangely absent in daily prayers. They are implied in the extended *Shema*, the most important prayer in Judaism, *"... these words shall be on your heart ...'* (Deuteronomy 6:4-9), but the commandments themselves are not recited. But what of the rest of our cultural landscape?

If you look hard enough you will find them. Many old churches, for instance, display them on dusty neglected walls. There are also many displays on walls throughout the USA. Unfortunately, in the current cultural climate, this has become an issue to some. In July 2017 a monument dedicated to the Ten Commandments was installed in the grounds of the Arkansas State Capitol, in the USA. Less than a day later the three-ton structure was smashed into smithereens by 32-year-old Michael Tate Reed II, who smashed his car into it, shouting "Freedom" to his Facebook supporters watching live! Immediately a funding account was set up by the producers of the movie "God's Not Dead" to pay for the rebuilding.

Why the controversy? Some say it is to honour the country's religious heritage, others say that it violates the separation of Church and State. A decade earlier a similar monument had been installed in the Texas Capitol grounds and deemed a correct act by the Supreme Court. This monument had been placed in 1961 by the Fraternal Order of Eagles, with the support of Cecil B. DeMille, the director of the iconic film, *The Ten Commandments*, with Charlton Heston in the starring role. In the Arkansas case a defender stated the fact that, since the founding of America, the Ten Commandments have played a historic role in the foundation of law in their free society. Apparently not all agree, or at least don't consider it relevant in today's political climate.

In 2018, a Ten Commandments plaque was removed from a park in Ohio, USA after complaints from an atheist group, who stated it was unconstitutional, and that it prohibits the worship of other gods (as if they cared!). This drew a backlash from Hendrik Storm from the Barnabas Fund, who declared:

"The United States of America was founded upon and guided by Judeo-Christian principles and these form the moral basis of the American Constitution. Furthermore the Ten Commandments were well-known by all the founding fathers, and were assumed to be the basis of morality, and not an endorsement of religion by the State. Consequently it was etched in many places in the building that houses the US Supreme Court. Laws cannot be passed requiring particular religious beliefs as per the Constitution, but this does not negate having a basis of morality anchored in the Ten Commandments. We urge the city to reconsider its decision."

In the USA the debate has even reached the classrooms. In 1978, the Kentucky state legislature passed a law requiring the Ten Commandments to be displayed in every public school, in order to *honour a fundamental legal code of Western Civilization.* This law was challenged in court as violating the First Amendment of the U.S. Constitution, which states that no law can be made "respecting an establishment of religion." Supporters of the law pointed out that the system of laws in the USA is based on these Commandments and that it is important for students to learn about them. So, is this true? How much do the current legal systems in the UK and the USA owe to the Ten Commandments? A lot. Are they viewed as just relics of the past? Unfortunately, yes.

In 2010, Tina Dupuy, a nationally syndicated columnist, decided to "settle the case against the Ten Commandments" by trawling through the Constitution of the United States and deciding which of the Ten Commandments, if any, are referenced. She ended up with a score of 3.5 out of 10. She totally dismisses the first five Commandments, stating that the Constitution does not favour one God over any other, has no prohibitions over the worship of images, blasphemy is not covered by the clauses regarding freedom of speech and gives a half mark to the Sabbath laws, mischievously downgrading the score because of the change of day from Saturday to Sunday. She also states that there are no clauses protecting the rights of parents. She concedes ground to the Commandments regarding murder, stealing and false witness but suggests that a blind eye is offered to adultery and coveting, the latter surely the oil that greases the cogs of the American capitalist culture!

The secular argument insists that even the three *included* Commandments are not exclusive to Christianity and deny that the founding fathers based the Constitution on the Bible. They base this on the fact that the words "God", "Jesus" and "Christianity" don't appear anywhere in the document, nor does any language that could be deemed religious. This is a good example of placing *form* higher than *function*, concentrating on facades and semantics but neglecting the underlying mindset behind the writing of such an important document.

One way of viewing the Ten Commandments is as an alternative legal system, with just ten laws, to the existing United States law, with over 60,000 pages of laws printed in 45 volumes! The former, set in stone, is unmoveable and therefore intended to be timeless and relevant to all generations. The latter, crafted by flesh and blood, is ever expanding and subject to increasing interpretations. We like to make things difficult for ourselves!

It is interesting that these issues generate a lot of hot air in the USA, where there is a separation of Church and State, creating fault lines between the two, separating passionate supporters of each position. There is barely a glimmer of controversy in England, where the Church and State mix uncomfortably within the hotchpotch of confusion known as the Church of England.

In a 2017 YouGov poll of British people, the results indicated that the majority view was that only six out of the Ten Commandments were principles worth living by. As expected, it was the last six, the man-centred ones, that were voted for. 93% of those polled agreed with not committing murder or stealing, 87% were against false testimony, 73% adultery, 69% against dishonouring parents and 61% against coveting. God got a hammering here, with only 31% against worshiping false idols, 23% against using the Lord's name in vain, 20% agree to have no other god and 19% keeping the Sabbath (Sunday) holy. Believe it or not *even the Christians in the poll agreed that those particular four were not relevant today!* This is a sad indictment of the current church and something we will examine in more detail in the next part of this book.

But, before we go there, a warning sign. It has just been reported that Chinese authorities are instructing the State-approved "Three-Self" churches to replace the Ten Commandments with quotes from Xi Jinping, the President. Currently this has been implemented in the Luoyang region, perhaps as a 'pilot scheme', with the overall strategy of *sinicizing* ('Chinese-ing') Christianity. A lot of the new 'material' is to be taken from a speech he made in 2015! Sometimes truth can really be stranger than fiction ... and far more frightening.

PART THREE
The Reclaiming

Transitioning

No, this is not a nod to the murky waters of gender fluidity but rather a sad Christian reality. It is a false reality experienced by those Christians who are told that the New supersedes the Old but are never told *why or how?* What to do with the *Torah*, specifically the Laws of Moses and particularly the Ten Commandments? *We are under grace not law! Jesus has done away with the law!* You've heard these before but consider their implications. Is this a cause for "Christian" lawlessness? Are we Christians so "holy" that we no longer need guidelines to live by? Many think so, influenced by "teachers" who "know so"! There's a word for this, *antinomianism.* With the meaning "anti law", it was first used by Martin Luther in the 16th Century as an insult against those who believed that the sole purpose of the Law was to drive us to the Cross. It is conviction-free Christianity, blind to our faults and ignorant of the fact that we still have an inclination to sinful behaviour, which still needs to be personally dealt with. We have not become *sinless beings* and we still need Law to remind us so.

These people would look at Ephesians 2:8-9:

For you are saved by grace through faith. And this is not from yourselves, it is the gift of God: it is not from works, so that not anyone could boast. (Ephesians 2:8-9).

This is their thinking; *As Scripture tells us that we are saved by grace alone, then we can basically do what we like afterwards, as our works are not going to keep us from heaven.*

We need to understand this 'Blessed Assurance', God's promise to all true believers of the eternal life that awaits them. For every *true* believer this is a given, but sadly there are many false believers out there, who haven't totally given their lives over to God, who show no outward signs of being born again in the Spirit. For these people the 'Blessed Assurance' is not a reality and it is the responsibility of the Church to re-align them to the true path before it is too late! This is a joint enterprise and highlights the need for true discipleship of all who profess a faith.

For *true* believers we must ensure that we live in the assurance of salvation. David Andrew puts it most eloquently in this extract from his editorial in Sword magazine (Jan/Feb 2020).

"Salvation is not the terminus, it's the embarkation point. The journey is sanctification, which is better understood as 'salvation underway'. Jesus has paid the fare (in full) and there is no more to pay to reach our destination. In fact, we have already crossed over from death to life, have already been cleared and freed from God's judgment. At Calvary *"the chastisement that brought us peace was upon him"* (Isaiah 53:5 cf. Romans 5:1). *All condemnation has been lifted from us* (John 3:17; Romans 8:1) and *nothing can separate us from the love of God in Christ Jesus* (Romans 8:35-39). *"There is no more for heaven now to give"*. This means that **we are disciples, but we are not probationers** – there is no question over our final status, but along the way we shall learn many hard lessons about obedience and perseverance… "

As disciples we have a responsibility to God and to the Church. We must find our function and run with it. Unfortunately, many in the Church follow the thinking of *antinomianism*, that we are totally under grace and not law, a consequence of the teaching of *Covenant Theology* and the idea that Christ freed us from any responsibility for our behaviour – freeing us from any need for discipleship! This is a disconnect, brought about through the toxic consequence of the pagan understandings of Platonism that has infected the Church for centuries. It's the dualism that encourages an unconscious separation between our beliefs and our behaviour. Beliefs and doctrines must feed our faith and thus determine our actions and we will allow the apostle James to remind us.

"And you must steadily be doers of the Word and not only hearers, deceiving yourselves. Because if someone is a hearer of the Word and not a doer, this one is like a man when he observes his own natural face in a mirror: for he observed himself then went away, and immediately forgot what manner of person he was. But the one who looked into the perfect Torah the one of freedom, and continues to do so, not being a forgetful hearer but being a doer of work, he will be blessed, happy in what he does." (James 1:22-25).

"For as the body is dead without a spirit, so also faith without works is dead." (James 2:26)

The fact is that Jesus gave more laws to live by than Moses did, and many of them are tricky to keep as he sometimes adds his own conditions to them. For a full analysis of this please read my book, *God's Tapestry.* Paul mentions the continuation of the Law here:

Carry each other's burdens, and in this way you will fulfill the law of Christ. (Galatians 6:2)

The Law of Christ, eh? So Moses wasn't the only law-giver then? In fact, Jesus repeated nine of the ten commandments, (even adding to them where necessary) and demonstrated the other commandment, *keeping the Sabbath,* as something as still alive and kicking! Jesus addressed the situation generally in this famous passage in Matthew:

Hearing that Jesus had silenced the Sadducees, the Pharisees got together. One of them, an expert in the law, tested him with this question: "Teacher, which is the greatest commandment in the Law?" Jesus replied: "'Love the Lord your God with all your heart and with all your soul and with all your mind.' This is the first and greatest commandment. And the second is like it: 'Love your neighbor as yourself.' All the Law and the Prophets hang on these two commandments." (Matthew 22:34-40).

It's so simple really, Jesus really is so unlike many of our theologians who seem to revel in over-complicating everything and pander more to their own egos. Thank goodness they are not all like that and I am privileged to have the acquaintance of Bible teachers at our Foundations conferences who dig deep into the Word in order to present God's truth to others.

Jesus is, in essence, saying here;

if you truly loved me with all your heart, soul and mind then you would keep the first five commandments without question, if you loved your neighbour then you would do the same for the rest of the ten commandments. No question! He also addressed the situation specifically.

1. **"You shall have no other gods before me."** (Exodus 20:3).

Jesus said to him, "Away from me, Satan! For it is

written: 'Worship the Lord your God, and serve him only.'" (Matthew 4:10).

2. *"You shall not make for yourself an image in the form of anything in heaven above or on the earth beneath or in the waters below. You shall not bow down to them or worship them; for I, the LORD your God, am a jealous God, punishing the children for the sin of the parents to the third and fourth generation of those who hate me, but showing love to a thousand generations of those who love me and keep my commandments."* (Exodus 20:4-6).

"God is spirit, and his worshipers must worship in the Spirit and in truth." (John 4:24).

3. *"You shall not misuse the name of the LORD your God, for the LORD will not hold anyone guiltless who misuses his name".* (Exodus 20:7).

"This, then, is how you should pray: "'Our Father in heaven, hallowed be your name ..."'" (Matthew 6:9).

4. *"Remember the Sabbath day by keeping it holy. Six days you shall labor and do all your work, but the seventh day is a sabbath to the LORD your God. On it you shall not do any work, neither you, nor your son or daughter, nor your male or female servant, nor your animals, nor any foreigner residing in your towns. For in six days the LORD made the heavens and the earth, the sea, and all that is in them, but he rested on the seventh day. Therefore the LORD blessed the Sabbath day and made it holy."* (Exodus 20:8-11).

"For the Son of Man is Lord of the Sabbath." (Matthew 12:8).

5. *"Honour your father and your mother, so that you may live long in the land the LORD your God is giving you"*. (Exodus 20:12.)

"Jesus replied, "And why do you break the command of God for the sake of your tradition? For God said, 'Honour your father and mother' and 'Anyone who curses their father or mother is to be put to death.' But you say that if anyone declares that what might have been used to help their father or mother is 'devoted to God,' they are not to 'honour their father or mother' with it. Thus you nullify the word of God for the sake of your tradition." (Matthew 15:3-6)

6. *"You shall not murder."* (Exodus 20:13).

"You have heard that it was said to the people long ago, 'You shall not murder, and anyone who murders will be subject to judgment.' But I tell you that anyone who is angry with a brother or sister will be subject to judgment." (Matthew 5:21-22)

7. *"You shall not commit adultery."* (Exodus 20:14).

"You have heard that it was said, 'You shall not commit adultery.' But I tell you that anyone who looks at a woman lustfully has already committed adultery with her in his heart." (Matthew 5:27-28)

8. *"You shall not steal."* (Exodus 20:15).

"Why do you call me good?" Jesus answered. "No one is good—except God alone. You know the commandments: 'You shall not murder, you shall not commit adultery, you shall not steal, you shall not give false testimony, you shall not defraud, honour your father and mother." (Mark 10:18-19)

9. *"You shall not give false testimony against your neighbour."* (Exodus 20:16).

"They are not of the world, even as I am not of it. Sanctify them by the truth; your word is truth." (John 17:16-17)

10. *"You shall not covet your neighbor's house. You shall not covet your neighbor's wife, or his male or female servant, his ox or donkey, or anything that belongs to your neighbor."* (Exodus 20:17).

Then he said to them, "Watch out! Be on your guard against all kinds of greed; life does not consist in an abundance of possessions." (Luke 12:15).

So let's not be under any illusion that Jesus has ushered in an age of "sanctified lawlessness", under whatever name you would use for it. The *Torah* still exists. Jesus may have fulfilled the conditions within it for righteousness before God (Matthew 5:17-18), but we now have a *Torah* within our heart:

"This is the covenant I will make with them after that time, says the Lord. I will put my laws in their hearts, and I will write them on their minds." (Hebrews 10:16).

This is the work of the Holy Spirit within us, encouraging us to obey God's laws out of love for Him and His plan for us rather than ignoring them out of some mis-taught nonsense about 'living under grace' being a metaphor for *'you're saved now, so do whatever you want to do!'*

Now let's repeat the list, but this time, compare the new with the old, the Sinner's Charter followed by the World, with God's timeless truths ...

1."You shall have no other gods before me." (Exodus 20:3).

You can have as many gods you like, as long as you don't encourage others to believe as you do.

2."You shall not make for yourself an image in the form of anything in heaven above or on the earth beneath or in the waters below. You shall not bow down to them or worship them; for I, the LORD your God, am a jealous God, punishing the children for the sin of the parents to the third and fourth generation of those who hate me, but showing love to a thousand generations of those who love me and keep my commandments." (Exodus 20:4-6).

Feel free to place your affections and favour anywhere you like, as long as you don't hurt or disrespect anyone. Whatever decision you make is yours and yours only and it is not up to anyone else to pass judgement on your choices.

3."You shall not misuse the name of the LORD your God, for the LORD will not hold anyone guiltless who misuses his name". (Exodus 20:7).

We must learn to respect each other in words as well as actions, so we must be careful how we speak, otherwise we may be (perhaps unwittingly) committing an offence against society and be dealt with accordingly.

4."Remember the Sabbath day by keeping it holy. Six days you shall labor and do all your work, but the seventh day is a sabbath to the LORD your God. On it you shall not do any work, neither you, nor your son or daughter, nor your male or female servant, nor your animals, nor any foreigner residing in your towns. For in six days the LORD made the heavens and the earth, the sea, and all that is in them, but he rested on the seventh day. Therefore the LORD blessed the Sabbath day and made it holy." (Exodus 20:8-11).

Work, rest and play. You have freedom to choose what works for you, but you also have a responsibility for your family and your sense of self-worth to be a good citizen and help support the economy. No day is extra special and no-one has the right to impose their ancient traditions on your daily life.

5."Honour your father and your mother, so that you may live long in the land the LORD your God is giving you". (Exodus 20:12).

Do what seems best for your parents, at all times, but rest assured that society can ease the burden of an aged relative, so trust it to look after your loved ones in a satisfactory manner.

6."You shall not murder." (Exodus 20:13).

You must not kill another regardless of the circumstances and seek to preserve life as society defines it, unless personal freedom compels you otherwise.

7."You shall not commit adultery." (Exodus 20:14).

Be discreet in your relationships, so that as few people as possible would be affected by your

actions. Of course, society has no right to judge on these personal issues.

8."You shall not steal." (Exodus 20:15).

Stealing of possessions is an offence against society and should be duly punished. The stealing of human beings is also wrong and ought to be punished if possible.

9."You shall not give false testimony against your neighbour." (Exodus 20:16).

Fake News is indeed the scourge of our times but sometimes we need to follow the narrative and take into account different interpretations of an event. Nothing is ever black and white, truth is an ever-moving target, it is not an absolute.

10."You shall not covet your neighbor's house. You shall not covet your neighbor's wife, or his male or female servant, his ox or donkey, or anything that belongs to your neighbor." (Exodus 20:17).

There is nothing wrong with having the ambition to strive to legally acquire what you don't have. There is nothing wrong with fulfilling your desires.

So how is this going to work out for Christians? Will it end in tears or are we going to do something about it? Are the Ten Commandments for *today's Christian,* let alone today's society? What would Jesus want us to do, bearing in mind that he didn't annul any of them? How would he want us to relate to them?

It's time for a revisit …

God's first word – Only

Before we embark on the first of the "ten", we should pay attention to the pre-amble.

And God spoke all these words: "I am the LORD your God, who brought you out of Egypt, out of the land of slavery." (Exodus 20:1-2).

Even now, countless centuries later, He is *still* the Lord your God, who brought (the Israelites) out of Egypt. Times change, He doesn't. History may have moved on and He may have acquired new labels in our minds, in terms of His mighty deeds, such as *"I am the LORD your God, who rescued you from the World, out of slavery to sin"* or the historically accurate, *"I am the LORD your God, who sent my Son, My only Son, to die for you so that you may live"*. These are His calling cards, His USPs (in marketing parlance – Unique Selling Points), they set the scene for what is to follow. We must not forget this.

In my book *Into the Lion's Den* I recounted an unsettling but significant television event, an episode of ITV's *This Morning*, when the broadcaster Philip Schofield was castigating Andrea Williams of *Christian Concern*, for her "out of date" and "non-inclusive" views on the LGBT+ issue. The heart of the real issue was encapsulated in these words that he wielded like a weapon, *"… because that is not the way now that we are led to believe …"*

"… because that is not the way now that we are led to believe …"

This begs a question. *Who* is doing the leading here? Who is Schofield deferring to? Who makes the rules? This is a major question, one rarely asked but perhaps the question we should all be asking. That's the killer, the vast chasm that separates the Sinner's Charter from the Ten Commandments. It's all about *provenance,* a term used in the art world to determine the authenticity of a piece. The Ten Commandments have a clear historical provenance, the Mind of God, communicated to Moses and the Hebrews through the Finger of God. And what about the Sinner's Charter? A clever forgery, if the truth be told. Trouble is that the truth has little to say about it. It is a moveable, fuzzy, amorphous mass of public opinion, spin doctoring, fake news, rumour and gossip that appears to have a life of its own but I think we'll be surprised to know that there are master puppeteers at play here, *spinning and delving.*

We are led to believe. Those doing the leading are the self-named progressives, always taking us "upwards and onwards", never staying still, otherwise we would catch our breath and start wondering where this is all going. We have already met these people during our story, they are the ones who insist they are progressing to some ideal liberated society. This is a giveaway of course to the Marxism that runs at the heart of these ideas, a political theory that promises 'nirvana' but brings only misery, death and destruction, as witnessed in Soviet Russia, Communist China, North Korea and Venezuela. They promise "equality", "equity", "empowerment", "diversity" and "entitlement" but have served only to lower moral standards in our language and behaviour and have redefined the word "tolerance" to mean *believe what we tell you to believe in, or carry on in your intolerance.* By their standards there is no-one more "intolerant" than a

Biblical Christian, someone who doesn't believe that all religions lead to God and that there are only two sexes, because that is what God has created.

So Exodus 20:1-2 reminds us who is the Author of the Ten Commandments, Someone who we can trust, rather than some faceless influencer, operating from an unanchored soul. That is the Foundation that ensures that all that is built on it is true and eternal, rather than on shifting sands that can support nothing.

Now that we can see the contrast between the eternal Ten Commandments and the ever-morphing Sinner's Charter, we can begin to re-examine the Ten Words and decide what is relevant for Christians living in the 21st Century.

"You shall have no other gods before me." (Exodus 20:3).

Has become ...

You can have as many gods you like, as long as you don't encourage others to believe as you do.

Can we live with this? Can we accept this?

If we believe that the Ten Commandments are still valid for Christians, then we must accept that the rules haven't changed. The commandment accepts that there are "other gods" but utterly prohibits us to consider them in any way.

How have Christians fared on this issue? Have we knowingly – or unknowingly – given credence to "other gods"? We can look at the major religions and see how they have subtly polluted the pure Christian faith. This may be surprising to you.

Firstly, Allah of the Muslims is *not* the God of Abraham, Isaac and Jacob. Judge yourself from the following quotations from the Quran. *"For Christians, Jesus is certainly*

God and for Muslims Jesus is certainly not God" (5.72).
"Rebuke Jews and Christians for calling God their loving father because humans are just things that God has created."(5.18).

This means that any acknowledgement of Allah as God in conversation or prayer is giving credence to "other gods". One such initiative is *Chrislam* (a bit more catchy than Islach), which seeks to find commonality between the two religions. The first time this was tried was when the Church Fathers, in the 2nd Century, merged the pagan philosophy of Platonism with the Biblical gospel, in order to make Christianity "more favourable" to the pagans living in the Greek world of the day. This was an utter disaster and the end result was *Christendom*, State Christianity, that gave us the Crusades, Inquisition, persecution of the Jews and other Christians, doctrine wars, ecclesiastical power structures, corrupt Popes, idolatry and superstition. Two thousand years of 'what could have been' as a result of bad decisions made by those early Gentile believers. Of course, God still preserved the True Church during that time, through such people as the Waldenses, Hussites, Moravians and Methodists, otherwise you wouldn't be reading this and I wouldn't be writing this!

One controversial high-profile Christian leader who has persistently been linked with Chrislam is Rick Warren, author of *The Purpose Driven Church*. Internet rumours have abounded for many years declaring his compromising of his beliefs in order to reach out to Muslims in love. He has always denied this although he clearly used the Muslim name for Jesus (Isa) in his prayer at Obama's inauguration in 2009. Perhaps unwise in retrospect. Fairly recently, he issued a statement flatly denying rumours about him: "The rumour is 100 percent false," he wrote at Pastors.com, a website he founded that provides practical advice to church leaders. "My life and ministry are built on the truth that Jesus is the only way, and our inerrant Bible is our only true authority." Perhaps we should give Warren the benefit of the doubt, *but we are watching you, sir* …

In 2015, in the evangelical Wheaton College in the USA, Larycia Hawkins, one of its professors donned a hijab and wrote this on her Facebook page, *"I stand in religious solidarity with Muslims because they, like me, a Christian, are people of the book. And as Pope Francis stated last week, we worship the same God."* High intelligence, but little wisdom.

Sonya Jay Walker made this observation in a recent web article for independencedaily.co.uk:

"An Anglican church in southern England held a joint birthday celebration for Jesus and Mohammad which ended with an Islamic prayer. In Southern Italy, a parish priest actually produced a Muslim crèche, starring Mary in a burka and Joseph as a North African Muslim while another Italian priest eliminated the Christmas nativity scene outside his church 'because it could offend Muslims', and Islamic songs accompanied Christian ones in Florence's Cathedral. But possibly the most worrying of the Christmas services was that held in an Episcopal Church in Scotland because this included a reciting in Arabic of verses from the Koran which denied the deity of Christ which is of course, the whole point of the New Testament of the Bible."

It's not that Chrislam, or any related initiative, is doomed to failure, rather that those who are sucked into it are ensuring their own failure, on the basis of the First Commandment, so stay away because God, our Creator and Redeemer, deserves a lot better!

The progress of Hinduism into Church activities has been more subtle. The Yoga *asanas*, or body positions, retain elements of their earlier spiritual meanings. For instance, the *Surya namaskar* is a series of positions designed to greet *Surya,* the Hindu Sun God. They are positions of worship to a Hindu god. Some may argue, is it true worship if you are unaware you are doing so? Best not to put this to the test and surely it is best to err on the side of caution and holiness.

Here's what I wrote in *Livin' the Life*:

> It's the covert side of it that we need to be most wary of, the spiritual undercurrents that sway the undiscerning mind and drag it into bad places. For instance, is yoga harmless? How many church halls host yoga classes or martial arts classes or "Christian" mindfulness sessions? Does this make it OK, just because the local vicar has been swayed by these unseen forces and condoned these practices (usually for financial reasons)?

So, what should we do? First let's gird up our loins with Scripture, our anchor when the madness of our World encroaches: *The Spirit clearly says that in later times some will abandon the faith and follow deceiving spirits and things taught by demons. Such teachings come through hypocritical liars, whose consciences have been seared as with a hot iron.* (1 Timothy 4:1-2).

Some may argue that, as long as we are vigilant and alert, it is possible to indulge in some of these practices without being corrupted by them. Much discernment is needed here, to be able to sift the good from the bad. A warning should come from the fundamental principal of one of these practices itself, *homeopathy.* In this technique, a medicine is administered after the core ingredients are diluted so many times that there surely can't be more than a small clutch of molecules actually left in the mix when it is administered. This, apparently is not the point. The point is not the chemicals or molecules themselves, but the spiritual forces attached to them. And so it is with many of these "New Age" practices, one must look at origins and purposes and realise that there is always more going on than meets the eye. Don't let a pagan Trojan horse into your spirit. Be warned!

"You shall have no other gods before me." (Exodus 20:3)

We therefore need to be on our guard. Things may not always be what they seem. We need to hold onto the one truth that is going to get us into more and more trouble as the World "progresses" towards what could be a "one religion fits all" scenario. The truth is, that, as we have just read, there will be no gods before the God of Abraham, Isaac and Jacob but also that Jesus is the only way to God (John 14:6), a truth that is even more anti-progressive and counter-cultural … and hence dangerous!

God's second word – Worship

"You shall not make for yourself an image in the form of anything in heaven above or on the earth beneath or in the waters below. You shall not bow down to them or worship them; for I, the LORD your God, am a jealous God, punishing the children for the sin of the parents to the third and fourth generation of those who hate me, but showing love to a thousand generations of those who love me and keep my commandments." (Exodus 20:4-6).

This has become ...

Feel free to place your affections and favour anywhere you like, as long as you don't hurt or disrespect anyone. Whatever decision you make is yours and yours only and it is not up to anyone else to pass judgement on your choices.

We all worship, it's built into our natures. Its most basic definition is complete absolute submission to God. For most of the world it is not an issue, the act of worship is seen in trivial terms, but for Christians it is *a major issue*. If you're worshipping anything other than the Lord God, a wide-ranging punishment is promised.

So we need to get it right. First, we must think hard about what we mean by 'worship' in the first place. The following are ideas expressed in my book, *Hebraic Church*:

'Times of worship' have been traditionally deemed as musical interludes, led by the worship leaders on piano or guitar (or just voice). We warm ourselves up with a few repetitive choruses, perhaps with a hymn or two. Maybe some prayer and a Bible reading. When the musicianship and singing is good, we feel good. Is this because we feel *entertained?* Be honest. Does God feel *entertained?* Is this what it's all about? Is it about the quality of the sounds we make? This sounds cynical. Forgive me. But ...

We call this worship? So ... what is worship?

God is spirit, and his worshippers must worship in the Spirit and in truth. (John 4:24).

This is the verse that underpins it all. It emphasises the absolute solid bedrock of the truth, presented to us in Holy Scripture (*"sanctify them by the truth; your word is truth"*: John 17:17), personified by Jesus Christ (*"I am the way and the truth and the life ..."*: John 14:6) and illuminated to us by the Holy Spirit. Everything else follows from this.

It is where God's people meet their God. It is not localised, it doesn't need to be in a specifically ordained location, because God is everywhere.

And they were calling to one another: "Holy, holy, holy is the LORD Almighty; the whole earth is full of his glory." (Isaiah 6:3).

Let's look at a couple of scenarios from the Gospels. Firstly, we look at the reaction of Peter and the disciples after witnessing Jesus walking on the water.

Then those who were in the boat worshipped him, saying, "Truly you are the Son of God." (Matthew 14:33).

Did they whisk out a washboard and a penny whistle from their robes and beat out a rousing chorus? Then there's the blind man who was healed by Jesus with a lump of mud.

Then the man said, "Lord, I believe," and he worshipped him. (John 9:38).

Did he belt out a Psalm or two, accompanied by his parents, acapella-style? Probably not.

To get to the very heart of worship we need to understand the very heart of God. What does He want from us? This is simple and familiar:

Hearing that Jesus had silenced the Sadducees, the Pharisees got together. One of them, an expert in the law, tested him with this question: "Teacher, which is the greatest commandment in the Law?" Jesus replied: "'Love the Lord your God with all your heart and with all your soul and with all your mind.' This is the first and greatest commandment." (Matthew 22:34-38).

Therefore, I urge you, brothers, in view of God's mercy, to offer your bodies as living sacrifices, holy and pleasing to God - this is your spiritual act of worship. (Romans 12:1).

These may seem to be cherry-picked verses, but there are many others that I could have chosen that support the theme that God wants us to love Him and use all that He has given us, in worship back to Him. Instead the institutional Church, in its Greek thought-patterns, has transformed "worship" from a verb (a doing) into a noun (a thing). Or, more specifically, from a function to a form. Worship has become a packaged entity, even existing as a genre of music that's available as downloads or on metal discs.

… Now let's move into a time of worship …

Eh, aren't we already worshipping God? Is God just sitting there waiting for that first guitar chord to be struck, so that He can relax in the warm glow of receiving worship from a collection of vibrating tonsils?

There's no doubt that worship leaders and songwriters

have the best of intentions and are using their God-given gifts, but the problem is in the whole concept of considering "worship" as an entity, divorced from the One Who is to be worshipped. It is *form* replacing *function*. The *function* should always centre on God Himself and consider what He asks of us in our worship to Him.

To love Him and use our mind, body and soul in worshipping Him.

This is not only about singing choruses, though, of course, that is one expression of worship, if done properly with the best of intentions. But it's not the *only* expression.

Worship leaders perform their acts of worship through the writing and performing of songs that draw their hearts toward God. By doing so they are fulfilling the criteria just mentioned. Those who listen and are moved by these songs, are also sharing in this experience, but for these people, and for others who don't totally share in this particular experience, God is happy for them to worship in *other ways*.

... use our mind, body and soul in worshipping Him.

We weren't created just to be able to sing. We can also speak, read, study, argue, write, create works of art, build things, organise others, help others, clean a room, wash dishes … the list, of course, is endless.

For me, my main act of worship is what I'm doing right now (in my time frame, not yours). I'm writing these words which, for me, is a fulfilment of a pledge I made many years ago to God. As a writer, my career could have gone in all sorts of directions, but there was a point in time when I decided, *as my act of worship*, to direct all of my God-given talent back to the Giver of the talent. For me, writing is an act of worship. For you, perhaps you have made a similar promise concerning the talents you have been given, or perhaps you are still praying for a talent in the first place that you can return to the Creator with interest? We all have something of value, even if the World (or even the Church) doesn't recognise it as such, maybe because it doesn't fit in the usual grand mould of giftings. Your task is to identify it and offer it back to Him as your act of worship. Nothing is too little, or insignificant, as long as it is done with a willing heart.

... use our mind, body and soul in worshipping Him.

So, we need a wider concept of worship, a holistic approach which involves us giving back to the One who Created us. And it is different for each of us, because we are all uniquely different. Praise God!

So we should be clear now about the type of worship that God demands of us. This is fine if we are correctly aligned but, still, we have to remind ourselves of the warnings:

"You shall not make for yourself an image in the form of anything in heaven above or on the earth beneath or in the waters below. You shall not bow down to them or worship them; for I, the LORD your God, am a jealous God, punishing the children for the sin of the parents to the third and fourth generation of those who hate me, but showing love to a thousand generations of those who love me and keep my commandments." (Exodus 20:4-6).

Here are some traps that we could fall into.

Make of them what you will:

How we can fall into false worship:

• **Worshipping the worshippers**

That singer's dress is a little too revealing ... and I don't like the way he's holding his guitar ... that keyboard player has a strange way of singing, like she has marbles in her mouth ... don't think the drummer's washed his hair for weeks!

Of course, this is a bit of a parody, but there are probably crumbs of truth here. Worship groups can be a wonderful channel of guided praise ... but they can also be a distraction. We can end up concentrating on their form (looks / expertise / quirks) rather than their function and, in extreme cases where the form is most agreeable, great dollops of worship can be unconsciously (or intentionally!) rerouted towards them! Let's get real here. If sung worship is to be our primary way of acknowledging our God corporately then there needs to be no distractions. My advice is to site the worship group behind the congregation or behind a screen.

• **Building thrones for preachers / teachers / ministers / pastors**

Hey that charismatic American preacher is in town, speaking a few roads away. Let's skip our church and go and see what God has to tell us through him!

Why do we Christians copy the world in how we treat those who are following specific vocations? Many a pastor or preacher has been levered onto a pedestal and many of the same have been dramatically knocked down from one, if they haven't delivered the goods or *delivered the wrong goods*. The number of "clergy" who have risen to the top through their form (charisma, good looks, connections, forceful personality) rather than their function (actual giftings from the Lord) is worryingly high. You really get the impression that the Church largely follows the world's model in such matters, opening up paths through to the top for those with charisma, good looks, connections or forceful personality rather than an actual calling. Christians largely follow their favourite teachers, often endowing them with the same kind of devotion – *dare we say worship* – that is usually reserved for pop stars, film stars and assorted celebrities. But love can turn to hate if the "worshipped one" suddenly becomes undeserving, usually through past misdemeanours coming to light, as with Rolf Harris, Michael Jackson (allegedly) and a growing band of #metoo blowbacks. Christians who follow the same model can also be condemned by it and there's a huge number of fallen leaders, teachers and celebrities littering the ground, many of them not having the grace or self-awareness to retreat into anonymity and leaving behind disillusioned followers who realised they backed the wrong horse and should have given their wholehearted worship to God rather than one of His flawed earthly "representatives".

• Idolatry by any other name

You only have to follow the story of the golden calf (Exodus 32:4) to see how quickly worship can descend into idolatry. We can easily deflect worship away from God and towards religious objects, even Bibles. There's been many a zealot who has frowned on me for resting my Bible on the ground, as if I was knowingly disrespecting God Himself. It is a book, with words. The book itself isn't holy, though the words are. Idolatry can also arise when Christians, in extreme cases, focus – sometimes exclusively so it seems – on one aspect of their Christian journey. One example is extreme Christian Zionists who seem to look at the world through the lens of "what does this mean for the Jews and Israel" rather than the clear glass of the gospel of Jesus Christ. Other "good causes" include the environment, other people groups, creationism, End Times and so on.

So who are you worshipping today? If this is not an exclusive arrangement with the God of Abraham, Isaac and Jacob, then it may be time for self-examination.

God's third word – Name

18

"You shall not misuse the name of the LORD your God, for the LORD will not hold anyone guiltless who misuses his name". (Exodus 20:7).

This has become ...

We must learn to respect each other in words as well as actions, so we must be careful how we speak, otherwise we may be (perhaps unwittingly) committing an offence against society and be dealt with accordingly.

Mind your tongue! It's harder than you think when we begin to realise that casual blasphemy is endemic in our society, without an eyebrow raised to some of the most vile insults to our Creator God. What the World does is its own business, it is not up to us to judge. But we are free to pay a close inspection to Christian behaviour, both in general and specific to our closest Christian friends ... and, of course, ourselves.

So, thinking now about ourselves, are we condemning ourselves in our speech? It's serious business if we remember the example of these two chaps condemned by Paul:

... of whom are Hymenaeus and Alexander, whom I delivered to Satan that they may learn not to blaspheme. (1 Timothy 1:20).

Have we inadvertently committed grievous sins? Who am I to say? Who am I to judge? But we serve a God who forgives and it would be a good exercise if we all paused now and asked Him to forgive us for any past infractions on this issue. The thing is that we may also have to cover any future infractions because most of the words and phrases mentioned are so much a part of the English vocabulary, we probably are unaware when we are using them. But it's good to get before God on this and just assure Him that we'll do our best.

And it's important that we do make an effort, if we are trying to become more like Jesus and less like the mould that the World would like to force us into. Here's one for you young 'uns to set a good example to the rest of us:

Don't let anyone look down on you because you are young, but set an example for the believers in speech, in life, in love, in faith and in purity. (1 Timothy 4:12).

Our speech is one of our main interfaces with the World. Is our speech as clean as it could be?

"Don't you see that whatever enters the mouth goes into the stomach and then out of the body? But the things that come out of the mouth come from the heart, and these make a man 'unclean.' For out of the heart come evil thoughts, murder, adultery, sexual immorality, theft, false testimony, slander." (Matthew 15:17-19).

Whatever way you view it, perhaps, as Christians, our everyday language should reflect our beliefs. One word that ought to be used more is *blessing*, though it may seem a touch sanctimonious if over-used.

You're a blessed man! How blessed you are!

Perhaps there are better words we can incorporate into our speech?

But the fruit of the Spirit is love, joy, peace, patience, kindness, goodness, faithfulness, gentleness and self-control. (Galatians 5:22-23).

Do you have other alternative sanctified words that we can use? If so, please get in touch, it would be such a blessing.

It's just that what may seem trivial and irrelevant to us may actually *not* be so, but even irreverent to Him whom we love and follow. Isn't the point of loving someone (or Someone), the act of taking time to find out if you are pleasing or displeasing Them? Yes, there *have* been over three millennia since Moses came down that mountain with those stone tablets, and yes, we *are* living in New Covenant days, but if God instructed the Hebrews not to take His name in vain then, should that not also be so for Christians today?

Would you be disrespectful to a parent, a teacher, a friend's mother, your doctor or bank manager? You would be if you used their name in a casual curse. Would you look at a desperate situation and exclaim *Donald Trump* or *Piers Morgan*?! If you did it would seem odd, even comical, but crying *Jesus Christ* would not result in an eyebrow to be raised, although, in early days, we could have been facing a death penalty for blasphemy! If we truly love Him, shouldn't this make us cringe and pass comment, or isn't this appropriate in the current climate? By not passing comment wouldn't a very different message be conveyed? That we don't take our faith seriously enough? If we are brave enough to pass some sort of comment, we are reinforcing our belief that we are not just following a religion, but that, at the heart of this religion, is a relationship with a very real Divine Person and it pains us to hear Him disrespected so! This would be so 'left field' that, for some people, it is likely to get you more noticed than one of the traditional evangelistic approaches. It says a lot about a faith system if it doesn't just promote its central figure but that it gets very hurt when this Figure is insulted. Contrast this with Islam, which sends out warriors with bombs and machetes in response to any disrespect of their 'prophet'!

So mind our tongue we must, even if it means taking a moment or two before we speak. Better to seem considered and safe than rash.

We will end this chapter with an interesting news report:

> A town in northern Italy has introduced a fine for those who take the Lord's name in vain. The city council of Saonara, a town near Padua has introduced a law making it illegal "to blaspheme against any faith or religion" and utter foul language in public. The town has a population of 10,000 residents and anyone found in breach of the new law could find themselves facing a fine up to €400 (£360). The town's mayor, Walter Stefan, said the move was designed to get rid of uncivilised behaviour. Mayor Stefan told the Daily Telegraph: "With this law, you will not be able to cause offence to any religion, we have to respect the faithful." The mayor who is a practising Catholic, said it was designed to protect all faiths, not only Christianity.

Perhaps too little too late?

God's fourth word – Rest

"Remember the Sabbath day by keeping it holy. Six days you shall labor and do all your work, but the seventh day is a sabbath to the LORD your God. On it you shall not do any work, neither you, nor your son or daughter, nor your male or female servant, nor your animals, nor any foreigner residing in your towns. For in six days the LORD made the heavens and the earth, the sea, and all that is in them, but he rested on the seventh day. Therefore the LORD blessed the Sabbath day and made it holy."
(Exodus 20:8-11).

This has become …

Work, rest and play. You have freedom to choose what works for you, but you also have a responsibility for your family and your sense of self-worth to be a good citizen and help support the economy. No day is extra special and no-one has the right to impose their ancient traditions on your daily life.

Earlier, I wrote the following: It's the *function* of Sabbath that we must keep returning to, even if we remove the religious trappings. It is a *day of rest*. We need rest. We need time to take a breath, away from the rat-race, to enjoy friends and family. It's our society that sees us as economic units rather than human beings, as consumers rather than people. God saw all this coming, He reminds us continually through His eternal Word of the importance of rest, specifically a day of rest, preferably on the assigned day, the Saturday Sabbath but, if that isn't possible, any day is better than no day!

So Sabbath is generally a good thing because we are both following a direct command from God that He hasn't rescinded and enriching our family life through earmarking a day for rest and fellowship with man and God. Two thousand years of dodgy Christian history, misunderstanding and error have determined that the issue of the Sabbath is always going to be controversial and potentially divisive, particularly for Christians. One should always look beyond the façade and form and consider the function behind any situation. The volume of negativity thrown at the Sabbath indicates that surely it is a battleground with every possibility that most of the artillery thrown at it derives from an infernal abode, if you get my meaning.

How can Christians embrace this without being labelled as heretic, cultist or Judaiser by "traditional" Christians?

So let's say we are going to dip our toe in the water, just to get a flavour of what we may be missing. If there are blessings involved in obeying one of God's commands, then we should at least give it a go, there is really nothing to lose. Taking the 'minimum configuration', once we have set aside some time to do so (not necessarily a Saturday), there are two aspects to Sabbath, *what we say and what we do, the liturgy and the practice*. In all of this we must have our eyes on the *function* of the Sabbath, finding rest in each other and in the Lord, rather than getting bogged down in calendars, ritual or even accepted practices. Let's imagine that all we have as a guide is the Scriptures. Here are the relevant passages:

By the seventh day God had finished the work he had been doing; so on the seventh day he rested from all his work. Then God blessed the seventh day and made it holy, because on it he rested from all the work of creating that he had done. (Genesis 2:2-3).

This tells us that the Sabbath is a God-initiated enterprise. In fact, He was the first to keep it!

Remember the Sabbath day by keeping it holy. Six days you shall labor and do all your work, but the seventh day is a sabbath to the LORD your God. On it you shall not do any work, neither you, nor your son or daughter, nor your male or female servant, nor your animals, nor any foreigner residing in your towns. (Exodus 20:8-10).

Here the fourth commandment reminds us that the purpose of the Sabbath for us, is as a day of rest.

Then he said to them, "The Sabbath was made for man, not man for the Sabbath. So the Son of Man is Lord even of the Sabbath." (Mark 2:27-28).

When we read the context of this passage, Jesus is telling us that we should not be bound by man-made traditions on how we keep the Sabbath.

Therefore do not let anyone judge you by what you eat or drink, or with regard to a religious festival, a New Moon celebration or a Sabbath day. These are a shadow of the things that were to come; the reality, however, is found in Christ. (Colossians 2:16-17).

You act in the way you have personally been led. This means not judging others for not doing likewise and not being under judgement from those who disagree with you.

One person considers one day more sacred than another; another considers every day alike. Each of them should be fully convinced in their own mind. Whoever regards one day as special does so to the Lord. Whoever eats meat does so to the Lord, for they give thanks to God; and whoever abstains does so to the Lord and gives thanks to God. (Romans 14:5-6).

As long as you and God are on the same page!

So, armed with the Scriptural foundation, we are reminded that God both indulged Himself and asks us to consider this day as a day of rest, that we should not be condemned by either tradition or other people, as long as we are following God's specific leading, understanding that this may not be the leading for others.

So, to begin.

Laying aside the daily calendar we need to be convinced that this is to be a 24 hours period and that it should ideally start and end at sunset (*... there was evening and there was morning ...*). What happens between those two markers is up to you ... prayerfully, of course. But, even then, we must consider seasonal variations. In the UK, sunset can vary from 4pm (height of winter) to past 9pm (height of summer). If we were to stick to the form (Sabbath starts at sunset) then we are either going to have a very late supper, which could be problematic for the kiddies or a very early supper, not so good for those who commute to work. So, let's stick to the *function* (a time of peace and rest) and declare the start of the Sabbath *at a time that is convenient for you*. Let's not get too religious about this!

Here are some pointers you may want to consider:

You will need to develop a specific liturgy, that which works best for your family (Suggestions will be provided in the booklet, *The Sabbath Telling*, when published). This may already be something that you have developed together or perhaps this is a new thing. The idea is to spend a short time now in worship to the Lord, but doing so by using your own 'order of service'. You may wish to skip this step at first, but it would certainly be a good thing if this can be developed over time, with the agreement and involvement of all members of the family and, if possible, including every member of the family in the service itself, rather than the father doing all of the work. Here are some possible elements:

- Songs – either accompanied by guitar/piano, or unaccompanied, or singing along to a recording.

- Bible reading – perhaps a chapter from a Gospel or just a short passage or verse chosen by a nominated person (any member of the family).

- Short talk – just a few words – perhaps by the person nominated above, as a commentary on the Bible reading.

- Prayer – either a general prayer by the father or nominated person, or an open prayer time. Whatever works for your family.

- Confession/reflection – a quiet time when everyone considers their behaviour over the past week, particularly concerning attitudes to other family members. This could involve public proclamation, as long as this is not too awkward, so as to bring fear or resentment.

- A connection to the Sabbath heritage. Perhaps a group prayer based on Psalm 122:1 (*'Pray for the peace of Jerusalem'*) with a sincere and open-hearted plea for God's mercy towards Jewish people worldwide, particularly in the Land of Israel? It is strongly advised that this option should be considered. Apart from everything else it would be a wonderful witness to any Jewish people you know, that you are embracing their tradition (even if they are not doing so themselves) but with acknowledgement of its origins. On the flip side, running a Sabbath with no acknowledgement could be seen as one of the worst forms of *cultural appropriation*, theft from another culture!

These elements are optional and totally up to you, but it would be advisable to incorporate at least some of them, to build a spiritual foundation for the Sabbath as well as a show of unity and togetherness that will be carried through to the Sabbath itself. (Of course, you may, through a variety of circumstances, be 'running solo' but there's no reason why one couldn't enjoy the Sabbath as a single individual. With God on your side, you're never going to be really alone).

There is now an evening to look forward to, followed by a morning and afternoon. How do we fill this up in the spirit of Sabbath? What will we be doing that we don't normally do in the rest of the week? What will we, or won't we be doing?

Again, all I can give is pointers, but it is important to avoid any pitfalls that may invalidate the whole experience. And here's the biggest of them all:

The Mobile phone / cell phone / 'second brain'/ 'ever-present friend'.

In recent surveys 94% of millennials go online daily, mostly through their phone, spending around 7 hours a day consuming media! Yes, there was a day when these gadgets weren't glued to our hands and ears, but most of us can't remember this, although it was only a few years ago! How can your average family, let alone the addicted 'millennials' survive 24 hours without one? Because ...

Sabbath **HAS TO BE** a mobile-free zone, if it is going to work by encouraging us to rest and cut ourselves off from the distractions of the world outside the ring-fence. Phone calls / text messages / WhatsApp notifications / tweets / Facebook posts / Instagrams (and whatever's the 'new kid on the block' since going to press) are a constant source of anxiety, whether through receiving them, not receiving them or anticipating receiving them / not receiving them!

How are you going to cope? Here are two possible strategies:

1. Everyone in the family must relinquish control of their phone, placing it in a locked drawer and telling the outside world that the family can only be reached in the old-fashioned way, the land line, if there is an emergency.

2. If there is no land line or the first option doesn't appeal, then all the family must promise to operate as we all did in the early days of mobile phone technology, through 'pull' notifications rather than 'push'. In other words, we interact with the phone on our terms, rather than receiving ('pushing') a continuous stream of notifications. What this means is that all phones are placed in a single accessible location and, at set times, family members switch on their phone to check for emergency communications, which they can see at a glance. Just two minutes, then back to the day ...

Other distractions ...

They all seem to involve electricity and so perhaps we should envy the ultra-orthodox Jews who do not permit the use of electric devices at all on the Sabbath (unless they were switched on before-hand).

Computers

As the PC is the central focus of most work environments, it really has no place within a Sabbath, where a 'time of rest' has been specifically set aside to escape from work! Perhaps it can be covered by a cloth, so that it does not entice any family members into 'its world'.

Televisions

The average amount of time the average person spends in front of 'the box' (or 'the panel' as they are no longer box-shaped!) is far too large and is even worse if you add to it the hours people spend consuming TV/videos on their mobile phones. Yet there can be a place for it on a Sabbath, if there is a communal experience watching a suitable tasteful film or TV show. It doesn't necessarily have to have a worthy theme, or even a Christian one, sometimes we all need a bit of good clean mindless fun together as a bonding experience!

Christian TV is not always a good idea, unless a specific, suitable show is targeted. There is a lot of dross and inappropriate programming that can do more harm than good with indiscriminate viewing. Prosperity preachers loom large, particularly with the USA channels and should be avoided at all cost.

Radio/CDs

Good worship CDs are to be welcomed, as are worship channels on the radio. Christian Talk radio is best avoided, as it is unlikely that material would be appropriate for the whole family as we have to remind ourselves that, ideally on the Sabbath, we are looking for activities that all members of the family can feel comfortable with and that would serve to create a peaceful and restful environment.

'Hell and brimstone' preaching is not conducive to this, or even solid Bible teaching if it is pitched at a higher level than your kids' levels of comprehension.

So, what shall we do on the Sabbath?

Let's think, first, of the objectives for this day. Look at it as a little cushioned 'time' compartment, separated from the hours leading in and the hours leading out. It is a *holy* time, in fact it is the first thing 'made holy' in God's Creation (Genesis 2:3). It is as if time stands still within this compartment, kept apart from the hurly burly and distractions outside. And the purpose of this is to give a group of people, whether a biological family or 'spiritual' family, room to breathe in a safe, secure environment, free to enjoy each other and to connect individually and corporately with God.

One of the most contentious issues regarding Sabbath is the definition of "work", as in ***"on this day you shall not do any work"***. This is a clear example of form and function in action, where we discover that God is particularly interested in function over form. What this means is that we should concentrate on ceasing activities that fit the definition *"that which I do in order to earn a crust of bread"* rather than all activities per se. Does God really want us to go through logistical nightmares *on a day of rest* just to use electricity, or driving the elderly, or cooking? I very much doubt it. What He doesn't want us doing is monitoring emails, writing reports, taking business calls or discussing work-related topics with all and sundry. What He does want us to do is to enjoy Him and our close family without worrying over any possible infractions of man-made laws that surround the Sabbath.

For it to work, there needs to be a 'Sabbath' state of mind for every family member, where:

- What's happened in your working week has to stay in your working week. All issues relating to work need to be parked and re-joined after the Sabbath.

- Any issues your family members may have with each other are dealt with during the evening 'service time'.

- You enter the Sabbath with eager anticipation that God is going to meet with you all.

- You feel ready for a good rest, with fun and silliness and a real sense of 'letting your hair down'.

- Endeavour to make it an open house for family and friends, but only if they appreciate what this day means to you i.e. avoid disruptions and misunderstandings. By all means invite non-believers, if they have an open heart and mind, as we trust that this special period should allow God to touch them in some way.

A RECIPE

Here are some suggestions of things you may want to do during the Sabbath:

- Talk about everything or anything (non work-related of course).-Worship the Lord in the best way that fits with your family – pray, read the Bible together, listen to music, sing choruses etc.

- Eat in a leisurely manner – why rush on a day of rest?

- Peer over family photo albums.

- Give testimonies of what God has done for you over the last week.

- Thank Him publicly for the blessings of the previous week.

- Little afternoon snoozes (and why not, you can't get more restful than that!)

- How about an ongoing family Sabbath jigsaw?

Of course it all depends on your particular family distinctive. We are all different in character and approach to life, and so it is too with family groups. You may be a family that likes discussion and (healthy) argument. If so, here's a suggestion for you:

- Saltshakers (our parent ministry) emails out a weekly list of key news items and interesting and provocative videos. Why not use these lists to provoke a discussion among you – you can democratically vote on which one to use. You can sign up for these on *www.saltshakers.com*.

Or you may be a fun family that likes to keep things light. If so, how about this?

- Create a 'games box' filled with a collection of 'old fashioned' board games that people like me will fondly remember from our youth. Games like ludo, snakes and ladders, draughts, dominos, card games or perhaps get serious with Monopoly, Cluedo or Risk. You never know, you may get your kids drawn into this safe retro fare and help to wean them off their devices. (Some hope!)

Or, if you are both fun and serious, here's another suggestion:

- A treasure hunt. Take turns to run it every week.

Someone hides the 'treasure' (a small object, such as a bell) within the house in a very obscure place. They provide a clue (perhaps a short verse) to kick things off, that points to a separate location. When someone solves that clue, there will be a second clue found at this location. Solving this will take them to a third location, and so on. Do this for as many times as you like until the final clue actually leads to the treasure. Perhaps there could be a prize attached to it, such as a bar of chocolate!

Here are some suggestions of things that you *may not* want to do during the Sabbath:

- Leave the home – apart from a brisk walk perhaps, or a visit to another family who are also enjoying a Sabbath rest.

- Go to church – let "church" come to you!

- Indulge in anything that is an overflow from a "working week" – it's not a time for catching up with writing reports etc.

The end of the Sabbath

So the afternoon draws to an end and sundown approaches. It is time to say good-bye, farewell, Auf Wiedersehen to your family Sabbath and prepare for a return to the general hub-bub.

God's fifth word – Honour

"Honour your father and your mother, so that you may live long in the land the LORD your God is giving you". (Exodus 20:12).

This has become …

Do what seems best for your parents, at all times, but rest assured that society can ease the burden of an aged relative, so trust it to look after your loved ones in a satisfactory manner.

Here's a quandry. You have aging parents who are now very dependent on you. They are in reasonable health, so haven't entered the State care system. You are their care system. Problem is that you "have a ministry" and surely God's call on your life has to take priority. That is true but may not be the answer you are looking for when you realise what this calling entails.

And he continued, "You have a fine way of setting aside the commands of God in order to observe your own traditions! For Moses said, 'Honour your father and mother' and, 'Anyone who curses their father or mother is to be put to death.' But you say that if anyone declares that what might have been used to help their father or mother is Corban (that is, devoted to God)— then you no longer let them do anything for their father or mother. Thus you nullify the word of God by your tradition that you have handed down. And you do many things like that." (Mark 7:9-13).

Here Jesus makes it very clear how one should

interpret the Fifth Commandment. If you have aging parents, a significant factor of *God's call on your life* is to honour them by caring for them to the best of your ability and as circumstances allow. To truly honour them is to treat them as you would want to be treated, to give of your time and effort, not just to throw money at the "system" to care for them instead of you. Our society, as I said earlier, does tend towards the "nanny state", but it's not for benign reasons. We are encouraged to palm off responsibilities to others, to live a selfish existence caring for ourselves, with plenty of cash to consume goods and services we don't really need and thus feed the system. This idea was espoused by Plato, who encouraged parents to hand over their children to the State for their education. The State doesn't know the best for us and our families ... we do!

Let's look at the underlying function behind this commandment. Honouring one's parents can be expanded to honouring all those who have inputted into your life over the years, which could include foster or adoptive parents, grandparents, uncles and aunties and so on. But it can also include teachers, family friends, neighbours, ministers, even those in your peer group who you may have grown up with. The word I am grasping for here is one that has been massively hijacked by factions of society. The word is *respect*.

R-E-S-P-E-C-T warbled Arethra Franklin in her pomp, *Respect bro'* can be overheard in gatherings of urban youth and its opposite, *are you dissing me?* can also be heard on the streets, often menacingly. All of these definitions have, at their starting point, the notion that *my world is the most important thing to me* and anyone who is 'disrespecting' (dissing) me is committing a cardinal sin. It comes from the individualism of our society, mentioned earlier and conjures up an allied concept, that of *entitlement*. The whole package has produced a segment of society (not just urban youth) that insists their very existence is a fact that ought to command respect from others, whether or not it has actually been earned and that there's an entitlement that determines that everything must fall into place just to ensure that our band of individuals have a happy and contented existence.

That isn't how the world works. The problem is *other people*, particularly those who also demand respect and entitlement. Thankfully *most don't* and live lives that acknowledge and bounce off others, perhaps even with behaviour approximating to the Golden Rule of Scripture, quoted in many places, such as here:

So in everything, do to others what you would have them do to you, for this sums up the Law and the Prophets. (Matthew 7:12).

Of course, for Christians, it is all about other people. All the gifts God freely gives to us are for us to use to encourage others, teach others, heal others, minister to others and so on. So, whereas the Golden Rule is a good template for general use, we should be giving to others regardless of what we receive from them, or expect to receive from them. As for the question of respect, that should not be an issue for us. Instead:

Show proper respect to everyone, love the family of believers, fear God, honour the emperor. (1 Peter 2:17).

So, it's not about receiving respect, rather giving respect to others: Above all:

"Honour your father and your mother, so that you may live long in the land the LORD your God is giving you". (Exodus 20:12).

And entitlement? Here are a couple of quotes in the secular world that are quite telling:

"When we replace a sense of service and gratitude with a sense of entitlement and expectation, we quickly see the demise of our relationships, society, and economy." (Steve Maraboli, Unapologetically You: Reflections on Life and the Human Experience)

"Entitlement was, she knew, a terrible thing. It chained the person to their victimhood. It gobbled up all the air around it. Until the person lived in a vacuum, where nothing good could flourish." (Louise Penny, Kingdom of the Blind)

For Christians, what are we entitled to? See how Paul compares the life we leave behind with our new lives in Christ. No hint of entitlement here!

So I tell you this, and insist on it in the Lord, that you must no longer live as the Gentiles do, in the futility of their thinking. They are darkened in their understanding and separated from the life of God because of the ignorance that is in them due to the hardening of their hearts. Having lost all sensitivity, they have given themselves over to sensuality so as to indulge in every kind of impurity, and they are full of greed. That, however, is not the way of life you learned when you heard about Christ and were taught in him in accordance with the truth that is in Jesus. You were taught, with regard to your former way of life, to put off your old self, which is being corrupted by its deceitful desires; to be made new in the attitude of your minds; and to put on the new self, created to be like God in true righteousness and holiness. (Ephesians 4:17-24).

Living for others in righteousness and holiness. And if we are to respect and honour others, it is those closest to us that take priority:

Anyone who does not provide for their relatives, and especially for their own household, has denied the faith and is worse than an unbeliever. (1 Timothy 5:8).

Here it is in black and white. If we fail to keep the Fifth Commandment then we are worse than unbelievers and have denied the faith. In a cynical world, people are only too glad to see Christians fail and we are constantly being watched to see if our behaviour is a reflection of the One we claim to follow, Jesus Christ.

If we can't even treat our own parents with honour and respect, then surely there's nothing about us that is different and we might as well be unbelievers. In fact, many unbelievers treat their parents better than a few Christians I can think of.

God's sixth word – Murder

"You shall not murder." (Exodus 20:13)

This has become …

You must not kill another regardless of the circumstances and seek to preserve life as society defines it, unless personal freedom compels you otherwise.

Before the 1960s our society hardly balked at the thought of 'an eye for an eye', when cold-blooded murderers were strung up by their necks in retribution for deeds that deserved far more. Is it because we have become so humane, or is it that we have simply become detached from our roots? One of the earliest laws given by God to man made His views perfectly clear on the matter:

And for your lifeblood I will surely demand an accounting. I will demand an accounting from every animal. And from each human being, too, I will demand an accounting for the life of another human being. *"Whoever sheds human blood, by humans shall their blood be shed; for in the image of God has God made mankind"*. (Genesis 9:5-6).

This is God's Heart. He has never changed, but our society has. Whereas, just a few hundred years ago young boys were hanged for stealing a pig, we now reward mass-murderers and child-killers with free board and lodgings for life, consistent with our warped view of 'human rights', even for those who have scraped the depths of the pure evil of which humanity is capable. This is not justice, just humanistic nonsense dressed up in the garb of 'progressiveness'. And if you disagree then ask yourself why nearly a quarter of a million of all pregnancies in the UK were terminated in 2018? Our humane society is a 'wolf in sheep's clothing', content with believing that an unborn human being is worthless and casting a blind eye to the mass-murder committed in the name of 'women's rights', when abortions are performed as a lifestyle choice, rather than a medical one. What an upside-down world we live in! Thankfully, this is the world that God saves us from, when we transition from the 'Kingdom of the World' to His Kingdom.

Surely one of the goals of every Christian is to discern God's Will and then make sure our actions are consistent with it:

Do not conform to the pattern of this world, but be transformed by the renewing of your mind. Then you will be able to test and approve what God's will is—his good, pleasing and perfect will. (Romans 12:2).

This passage is key to what has gone wrong in society and in much of our Christian life in this country. We have not allowed the Holy Spirit to renew our minds, instead we have allowed the world to seduce us with its patterns, fashions, factions, actions, reactions and tractions.

How and when did all this happen? Well, there were two separate historical processes and they both came together in the 1960s. Firstly, there was a decline in the Church. Here's how I explained it in *"How the Church Lost the Truth"*.

"But the really bad stuff in the 19th Century was happening in Germany and I'm not even going to cover the anti-Semitic and racial theories developed there, that were eventually going to lead to the rise of Nazism and the Holocaust. I'm not even going to mention the dark, soulless deliberations of Karl Marx and Frederick Nietzsche. Instead we focus on a direct attack on the Word of God, the Bible, itself... by Christians!

One attack was on the Old Testament, led by Julius Wellhausen, a German professor of the... Old Testament! He took the five books of the *Torah* and using the full tools of Greek logic and understanding, completed the job first started by Philo nearly 2000 years earlier. He analysed the Holy Scripture from all angles – historical, social, literary – bar one – the evidence of a supernatural authorship – and sucked away all evidence of the Holy Spirit's work. He produced something called the documentary hypothesis, an attack on Moses as the author of the *Torah*, still with us today, courtesy of liberal Christians of all persuasions.

Another attack was on the New Testament. Another German, Hermann Reimarus, a Deist, was one of many who entered a quest for the historical Jesus, a Jesus with all "mythology" swept away, an anaemic Jesus who travelled around the Holy Land doing nice things and saying nice things. A Jesus of revisionist history, but not the Jesus of the Bible, the miracle-working prophet who died for our sins and who was miraculously resurrected.

Most modern liberal Christians, whether they know it or not, follow the ideas of a German theologian, who lived at the start of the 20th Century. Adolph Harnack was canny enough to discern that Christian doctrine was thoroughly infected by Greek thought. His solution was to throw out the lot and concentrate on three selected aspects of Jesus' teaching. He stressed the Fatherhood of God, the Brotherhood of Man and the value of the human soul. He desired to strip out the supernatural elements of Christianity, but emphasised what has become known as the "social gospel". It was man's reason put ahead of divine revelation. It was fed by new "advances" in science, particularly the theory of evolution that was now being used to prise God's fingers away from the only place the Deists found room for Him - the Creation.

Liberal Christianity now has a firm foothold in the modern Christian mind, thanks to the rise of rationalism, the new religion in our secular humanist society. Scientific apologists, helped by our secularised educational system, make their views so attractive so ... reasonable and it is a tragedy in today's Church that so many have just rolled over without a fight and allowed Aristotle to claim victory.

Liberal Christianity is the predominant Christian expression in the UK, a 'Christianity' that very much conforms with the World more that it probably even realises. When we reached the 1960s, such a 'Christianity' was ripe for a take-over! This came courtesy of the second historical process, a wholly secular one that started in the mid-nineteenth century, through the writings of Karl Marx. Marxism started off as an economic theory that resulted in the failed Communist regimes of the 20th Century, such as Soviet Russia. By the 1960s it had morphed into a cultural phenomenon, giving rise to a process that currently has our 21st Century society in a stranglehold of fear, restrictions, conformity, fake news and fake tolerance.

The central thrust of this new Marxism is the

promotion of a 'victim culture', of building a narrative whereby all of the world's ills are the fault of the prevailing culture, specifically white men working from within a Christian context. It began to roll out a series of 'causes', centring on those deemed to be 'victims', such as black people, women, homosexuals, native Americans etc. There seems to be a worthiness in this until one realises that these causes were just part of the context of Cultural Marxism. Anyone who dared criticise this process are condemned variously as homophobic, misogynists, Islamophobic, racist, sexist and so on. Most of all they are labelled as 'Fascists'. Whereas traditional Marxism set up the ruling class, the "capitalists", as the aggressors and the working class as the victims, Cultural Marxism takes the same pattern but tweaks it. In place of the ruling class we have the traditional Western 'Christian' society as aggressor and any number of 'marginalised' groups as 'victim'. One key idea here is that the aggressor is never allowed any leeway, any shred of compassion, or any way of redeeming itself. It must be destroyed. Surely we see here the primacy of the ideology rather than a real concern for the "victims" who are being "defended"? This may seem a cynical attitude for me to take, but imagine if I am right on this, how cynical it is for people to perpetrate an ideology that creates conflict for their own ends?!

Out of this, political correctness triumphs and engineers the rise of the 'nanny state' with increasing intrusions and restrictions on the grounds of 'health & safety' to whittle away at our freedoms. This is what the New Left are all about these days and, with particular hold on the media and the metropolitan elite elements of society (the 'chattering classes'), Cultural Marxism is beginning to succeed in its goal of a controlled, collectivist society.

One tactic is, to put it plainly, to confuse us all and make us begin to query aspects of life that had hitherto been unchanging and accepted. For instance, they want to move us away altogether from *binary thinking*. So, instead of black and white we have an infinite selection of greys, so that 'no one colour' is dominant enough to prejudice our thinking. 'Man and woman' is too binary, we need to look at the whole spectrum of genetical possibilities! You can start to see the impact this thinking has had on the modern world. For a more thorough examination of this, you may want to read *Into the Lion's Den*.

None of this, of course, conforms to a Biblical worldview but, sadly, many in the Church have been dragged into it. If we were to summarise Cultural Marxism into a single word it is this, *liberation*, albeit a false one. Supposedly freeing people from the "restrictions" of the Judeo-Christian structure of society would make them happy and fulfilled. *Women's-Lib*(eration), Animal Liberation, Liberation theology and the rest do nothing more than concentrate on conflict rather than resolution and do nothing to ensure a stable society. Taking it further, it is saying that man (and woman) are basically good, but oppressed by external structures, such as church or family, hindering them from reaching their true potential.

All of this is a million miles away from the absolute truth of Biblical principles, such as:

"You shall not murder." (Exodus 20:13).

In a recent novel by John Grisham, the main character kills someone in cold blood but offers no explanation. He is a war veteran who had experienced much death and suffering and was no stranger to rough justice. It turns out that he killed the man because he suspected him of having an affair with his wife. He was tried and offered no defence because he knew he was guilty of premeditated murder and accepted that he had to die. To him, the Sixth Commandment was a natural and valid law and he accepted its verdict. He died on the electric chair.

Yet society in the UK has moved on from then ...

Christian pacificism, surely an oxymoron, though some would argue otherwise. It's all down to worldviews, as we have already discussed. There's the Biblical worldview, borne out of the Jesus Mindset, where God's Word is precious, universal and timeless. Then there's the World's worldview, borne out of the prevailing philosophy of the day, which currently is a tussle between the rational but atheistic *secular humanism* and the irrational mess created by Cultural Marxism. Finally, there's the worldview of the 'compromised' Church that mixes up all three, with the Biblical worldview ever pushed backwards. Christian pacificism, that insists that Jesus wouldn't harm a fly and neither should we, comes from this synthesis.

They declare that he embodied a vision of life that was deeply pacifist, even though he never explicitly brought up the subject of warfare. It all revolves around their concept of love, quoting Jesus in Matthew 22 (*"You shall love your neighbour as yourself"*) and they declare that Jesus understood this concept as the summary of the Hebrew Scriptures. This seems rather narrow as, of course God's love is painted on every page, but there are other aspects of God that are equally important, namely His holiness and righteousness. These are conveniently ignored as this would take us into areas that are very far from pacifism and would basically destroy their arguments for 'peace at all costs'. They are being very disingenuous in their reading of Scripture, using the liberal lens that had been forged over the last couple of centuries to raise 'human rights' above God's Righteous standards.

Was Jesus a pacifist? He healed the Roman centurion's servant, without castigating him for his career choice. His followers owned weapons, something Jesus condoned, Peter even used a sword during Jesus' arrest. Weapons were necessary for self-defence and you wouldn't own one if you never intended using it to protect your loved ones.

So, when we return to the Commandment, *You shall not murder,* we must always consider context, which includes consequences of actions and justice and one of the most ingrained instincts placed within us, *our need to protect those whom we love.*

"You shall not commit adultery." (Exodus 20:14)

This has become ...

Be discreet in your relationships, so that as few people as possible would be affected by your actions. Of course, society has no right to judge on these personal issues.

Adultery has no stigma attached to it these days; it is very much a feature of our "progressive" liberated culture. For Christians it is a much bigger issue, as there are spiritual implications.

Jesus reiterates the origin of marriage in Matthew 19:4-5, but he adds the following observation in verse 6: *"So that they are no longer two, but one flesh. Therefore what God has joined together, let no one separate."*

One flesh is thus not just a random coupling, but a lifelong commitment. From God's perspective every true marriage will be that which He alone has 'joined together'. He sets the terms, He does the matchmaking. The terms and reasons are summarised in Ephesians 5:22-33:

"Wives, submit yourselves to your own husbands as you do to the Lord. For the husband is the head of the wife as Christ is the head of the church, his body, of which he is the Saviour. Now as the church submits to Christ, so also wives should submit to their husbands in everything. Husbands, love your wives, just as Christ loved the church and gave himself up for her to make her holy, cleansing her by the washing with water through the word, and to present her

to himself as a radiant church, without stain or wrinkle or any other blemish, but holy and blameless. In this same way, husbands ought to love their wives as their own bodies. He who loves his wife loves himself. After all, no one ever hated their own body, but they feed and care for their body, just as Christ does the church— for we are members of his body. "For this reason a man will leave his father and mother and be united to his wife, and the two will become one flesh." This is a profound mystery—but I am talking about Christ and the church. However, each one of you also must love his wife as he loves himself, and the wife must respect her husband."

Here we are given another reason for one flesh and that it is one of God's mysteries, one of those things we accept rather than analyse or meddle with. The complicated bit is that Christian marriage, one flesh, is a model of Christ and his Church. This has the air of something very important indeed, using the physical to describe the spiritual.

So the wife submits to the husband, not because the man is stronger or more important, but because it is a picture of the Church submitting to Christ. Although this concept is an affront to feminists and "progressives" it is mysteriously bound up in the relationship we have with our Messiah. It is a principle, not an expression of masculine abuse. The husband is called to be the head of his wife, to act on her behalf in decision making. This he must do out of love for her, not as a power trip. But again, it is a picture, this time of Christ as head of the Church, as loving saviour.

Christian marriage is therefore a union of one flesh as ordained by God with two aims, or functions. Firstly, as the mechanism for producing offspring and therefore ensuring that the human race doesn't die out. Secondly, to demonstrate in some mysterious way the relationship that Christ has with his Church and reminding the husband and wife of their responsibilities within this arrangement. Also, God has ensured that masculine and feminine physical attributes correspond to these roles, to ensure they are best equipped to carry them out.

And this brings us to an important point. To explain it best we will again look at the difference between form and function. Our Greek mindset, which is predominant in the Church as well as in society, concentrates on forms, on objects and concepts, without paying attention to any meaning attached to said objects. A Hebraic mindset, as typified by Jesus and Jews of Bible times, would consider the function, the purpose behind the object. In our society marriage is a form, an all-purpose term for people who wish to make an official commitment to each other. This should not bother us Christians if the context is outside of our jurisdiction. It will be just a form with a function of making a general commitment, even if this is in a single sex context. But the rubber really hits the road if the context is Christian.

The function of a Christian marriage is for it to be acceptable to God, not the Church. If God is not honoured, then He is being mocked, whatever a denomination may decide to do for the sake of "unity". What is more important is unity with God and His word and if one flesh is not for the purpose of producing offspring (if possible) and modelling the relationship between Christ and his Church, then it is not a Christian marriage and God most certainly isn't the matchmaker.

Christian marriage ought to be the shining beacon of Church living, as a wonderful example of commitment between two people for life, as well as their joint dedication to God. There are many such marriages that do just this but, for various reasons, there are many that do not. The worst-case scenarios headlines like these:

> Popular evangelist Jimmy Swaggart, under church investigation reportedly for adultery, tearfully confessed Sunday that he had sinned and he will leave the pulpit for an indefinite period – marking the second major blow to television evangelism within a year. (LA Times Feb 22 1968).

It's been three decades since the world found out about the 15 minutes she spent in a Florida hotel room with televangelist Jim Bakker. But Jessica Hahn says it's only been in the last two years that she's finally confronted her anger about what happened, and how it's affected the rest of her life. She says she's angry at Bakker, founder of the onetime PTL empire near Charlotte, for using his power and his image as a man of God to manipulate her, then a 21-year-old church secretary, into having sex. "He just believed that everybody should serve him because he was serving God," she said of Bakker. (Charlotte Observer Dec 16 2017).

These were very high-profile fallings-from-grace. It is interesting to know that both evangelists have been fully restored and their "empires" continue!

And closer to home …

> An Anglican vicar has been banned for life for having an intimate affair with a married parishioner who came to him for pastoral support. The Rev. Simon Sayers, who was a vicar for over 30 years, received a permanent ban from the Church of England through a disciplinary tribunal in the Diocese of Portsmouth last week. Sayers, who

pastored at a parish in Warblington with Emsworth, was already serving a six-year suspension in 2016 for two "sexual incidents" with a 16-year-old girl in 1995, which drew a police investigation at the time but no criminal charges were filed. (Christian Post Aug 5th 2019)

The World's press loves these stories. It helps them to sneer at the Church and declare that *you're really no different from the rest of us, so stop preaching to us!* Every story like these serves to undermine hundreds of positive stories of faithful and fruitful Christian marriages. Well, Jesus didn't say it was going to be easy!

"If the world hates you, keep in mind that it hated me first. If you belonged to the world, it would love you as its own. As it is, you do not belong to the world, but I have chosen you out of the world. That is why the world hates you." (John 15:18-19).

Remember what I said earlier: the function of a Christian marriage is for it to be acceptable to God, not the Church. For it to be acceptable to God then surely it should be as the Maker's instructions? If Christian marriages model Christ and his relationship with the Church (Ephesians 5:22-33) then, any deviation from the very best is going to do considerable harm to the Body of Christ.

It is time to get back to basics.

God's eighth word – Theft

23

"You shall not steal." (Exodus 20:15).

This has become …

Stealing of possessions is an offence against society and should be duly punished. The stealing of human beings is also wrong and ought to be punished if possible.

Here is the summary we reached at in an earlier chapter:

All that we have comes from God, whatever the World tells us. Whether it is money, good looks, family, or life itself, all has a single origin. This means that if we acquire anything unlawfully, outside the functioning of the laws of barter or commerce, then we are not stealing from a person … but from God Himself. And the consequences will ultimately be from God Himself! That is the function that lies at the heart of stealing, an *offence against God*.

Just think about it. Every paper clip and pen you take from the office, every shampoo sachet you take from the hotel … and every bag of loot you stole from the bank in your latest heist. It's all the same with God, the matter of degree may seem an issue, but it's the motivation of the heart that is the driving force. Just as lust can give way to adultery and anger to murder, then the inclination to steal small things can possibly give rise to guilt-free plunder on a much larger scale.

As Christians we are not usually inclined to bank heists or major plunders, (but maybe we are.) There are other ways we can steal from others and therefore become an offense to God. Firstly, we can steal *time*. In our Greek-influenced world, time is a highly-regarded and jealously-guarded commodity. *Time is money. Time flies. Time heals.* It is one of the main *forms* that control our lives, we in the West live our lives governed by the clock (in marked contrast to those who live by the looser definition known as 'African time'). However we Christians view it or use it, it is still something that can be stolen. We can steal from God in many ways:

- By nurturing the gossip grapevine and wasting time on 'tittle-tattle'.

- By overloading ministers with problems that we should be solving ourselves.

- By forging ahead on a project without specific Divine approval (the intention may be good, but the *timing* may be wrong – I have been a culprit many, many times!)

- By failing to discern your function within the Body of Christ and perhaps operating in a function chosen by others or by default because no-one else is doing it. Again good intentions may be keeping you away from the best use of your time within God's plan for your life.

- By indulging in activities organised by the Church that you feel are not Divinely-approved, but which you are supporting out of "unity" or "duty" or "giving encouragement".

Let's not waste time any longer. I've already lost skin cells and brain cells that I won't get back, just by writing this sentence. We are not getting any younger, entropy has its iron grip of inevitability upon us. Let's make the days count that we have left. God knows all of the days of our lives in advance:

Your eyes saw my unformed body; all the days ordained for me were written in your book before one of them came to be. (Psalm 139:16).

There are those who would want to steal time from you. Avoid them if you can, if you have discernment about this. These are people who flit from person to person asking for healing or illumination despite rejecting advice that is not to their liking. They are looking for reinforcement, not completeness (Shalom) and would not hesitate to feed from your own shalom in the process.

Our time is a gift of God and we need to come to a realisation of this before it is too late, when we are close to the end in regret, admitting, *what did I really achieve in my life?*

Of course, in terms of stealing, the commodity that first comes to mind is money. In the first instance, for Christians, whether you are a penniless missionary or millionaire philanthropist, every penny you own – even if it's the widow's mite – is a gift from God. You don't own it, it has been lent to you. He is watching you and deciding whether you are the best custodian for the millions of pounds / thousands of pounds / few pence that He has allowed to pass through your hands. What He expects from you is illustrated by this parable:

"Again, it will be like a man going on a journey, who called his servants and entrusted his wealth to them. To one he gave five bags of gold, to another two bags, and to another one bag, each according to his ability. Then he went on his journey. The man who had received five bags of gold went at once and put his money to work and gained five

bags more. So also, the one with two bags of gold gained two more. But the man who had received one bag went off, dug a hole in the ground and hid his master's money. "After a long time the master of those servants returned and settled accounts with them. The man who had received five bags of gold brought the other five. 'Master,' he said, 'you entrusted me with five bags of gold. See, I have gained five more.' "His master replied, 'Well done, good and faithful servant! You have been faithful with a few things; I will put you in charge of many things. Come and share your master's happiness!' "The man with two bags of gold also came. 'Master,' he said, 'you entrusted me with two bags of gold; see, I have gained two more.'

"His master replied, 'Well done, good and faithful servant! You have been faithful with a few things; I will put you in charge of many things. Come and share your master's happiness!' "Then the man who had received one bag of gold came. 'Master,' he said, 'I knew that you are a hard man, harvesting where you have not sown and gathering where you have not scattered seed. So I was afraid and went out and hid your gold in the ground. See, here is what belongs to you.' "His master replied, 'You wicked, lazy servant! So you knew that I harvest where I have not sown and gather where I have not scattered seed? Well then, you should have put my money on deposit with the bankers, so that when I returned I would have received it back with interest. "'So take the bag of gold from him and give it to the one who has ten bags. For whoever has will be given more, and they will have an abundance. Whoever does not have, even what they have will be taken from them. And throw that worthless servant outside, into the darkness, where there will be weeping and gnashing of teeth.' (Matthew 25:14-30).

The general principle here is to ask ourselves, *am I a good custodian of what God has given me?* Because, if I am not, is it not stealing from God, Who could have chosen someone else to provide a better return? God is not wanting anyone to get rich (despite what prosperity teachers teach and the Catholic church – and others – practise), He just wants souls for His kingdom, not the building of an earthly kingdom, whether it manifests as glitzy cathedrals, huge walled communities for Christian 'celebrities' or financial portfolios. Your second holiday this year could have financed a small evangelistic mission in your area that, if it only produced one fresh saved soul, would bring far more rejoicing in heaven than would your topped-up tan in the Maldives.

I do some work for a Bible teaching mission school for a major denomination. This denomination benefits from the kudos of a worthy ministry in its portfolio but it has yet failed to give a penny to my knowledge to finance it! Most of the financing has come from the head of mission, from his own secular income. This is despite the head of the denomination being recently outed as one of the richest pastors in the world, with a net worth of $39 million!

This is stealing from the Kingdom on an industrial scale and it is shameful. It is undoubtably one story among hundreds of similar ones and indicates a serious disconnect in the heart of the Body of Christ when it comes to the flow of much needed funds to those who really need it for Kingdom purposes.

"You shall not steal."

Just four words, but with countless implications. Whether we are consciously adding to our own personal universe at the expense of others, or depriving blessing or functions of others through our failure to give of time or money, it's all the same to God. All He wants is a functioning Kingdom, not a pale replica of the very worst that the World offers.

It's not too late for us to *do our bit.*

God's ninth word – Fake

24

"You shall not give false testimony against your neighbour." (Exodus 20:16).

This has become ...

Fake News is indeed the scourge of our times but sometimes we need to follow the narrative and take into account different interpretations of an event. Nothing is ever black and white, truth is an ever-moving target, it is not an absolute.

When does Faith News become Fake News? The malaise of relativism is not just an illness in our culture, it has also found 'spiritual' expressions too. Let's face it, every spiritual expression that is not grounded in the true Gospel of Jesus Christ is 'fake news'. And it can be of the most dangerous variety, if it has the appearance of truth.

... having a form of godliness but denying its power. Have nothing to do with such people. (2 Timothy 3:5).

The commandment, in its most basic sense, speaks of leading others astray and we can all be guilty of this, not just through the fibs, peccadillos and downright lies that sometimes escape through our lips in our daily interactions, but, more importantly, how we are communicating the Good News of Jesus Christ to others. There are problems within and problems without, because the tiniest bit of yeast can infect a whole batch, even if it got there accidentally.

Take the Jehovah's Witnesses, for example. They are only relevant to this discussion because of their seeming omnipresence on our high streets, shopping malls, train stations, with their big smiles, smart appearance, colourful stands ... and corrupt message! How many innocents have been lured into their web of deceit, delivered with earnestness but owing its origins to the darkest of places? Surely it is harder to correct subtle error received through the JWs, than to deliver the truth to an open, expectant, unsullied heart. They represent danger of the highest order because they talk our language and reference our Saviour, but their version of Christ is not the Son of God but a created being and therefore powerless.

Here is John 1:1, using the Jehovah Witness *New World Translation:*

In the beginning was the Word, and the Word was with God, and the Word was a god.

Here is John 1:1, using the *New International Version:*

In the beginning was the Word, and the Word was with God, and the Word was God.

The only difference is a single letter and a capitalisation but it's a monumental difference. The JW's take on Jesus, the Word, is that he is merely ... *a god.* 'Just one of many', is the implication, and the lack of a capitalisation signals the low esteem in which he is held by them.

Another verse that they twist is John 14:11, where the relationship between God and Jesus is stated:

I am in union with the Father and the Father is in union with me. (New World translation)

I am in the Father and the Father is in me. (NIV)

A Jehovah Witness believes that Jesus was just a human being, despite a whole swathe of Scriptures that say otherwise, a problem they side-track by producing their own "version" of the Bible that "re-interprets" all of the difficult passages. The next time you meet a JW, ask them to explain John 20:28, as their version seems to have made a "boo boo" here, with an acknowledgement that at least Thomas thought Jesus was God, even if Charles Taze Russell (the founder of the JWs) didn't!

In answer Thomas said to him: "My Lord and my God!"

But, seriously, their error concerning the Person of Jesus is so damaging that, by Biblical standards they are not even saved. Yet they have been promised heaven and eternal life (of sorts … if they have earned it!). They have been sold a dummy and we must pray earnestly for the hundreds of thousands of lost souls held in such a bondage.

So we have just seen an example of the danger of Christian *Fake News*, or *Fake Faith*, to which we can add the Mormons and others. But then we have the *danger within*, of the problems within our own camp, mainstream Christianity, that seems to have grown from a single worshipping group of believers in Acts 2, to a smorgasbord of spiritual spaghetti, with over 40,000 denominations, a number growing daily as there will always be clever chaps with bright ideas, a ready smile, a smooth tongue and a posse of gullible followers!

We are counter-cultural, we believe in absolute truth and that it is found in the Bible alone. Trouble is that we seem also to have many interpretations of *what the absolute truth is*, depending on which angle you view the Bible from. Here's what I said in *How the Church lost the Truth*:

Jesus did a lot of stuff. Virtually everything he did was to fulfil the words of prophets of an earlier age. He healed, he taught, he comforted, he corrected, he put people right with God. In doing so he was able to point to his actions as fulfilments to the writings of Isaiah, Jeremiah, the Psalms and many other places. He was able to do so because there was a general agreement among the Jews of his day as to what these Scriptures were saying. They knew how to make sense of their Scriptures. The question of interpretation was not an issue as they all shared the same tools for reading these sacred words. Not so today. Over the last 2000 years of Christianity we have developed so many ways of reading and interpreting the Bible, it seems that we can make Scriptures say whatever we want them to say, without any regard to what they are actually saying. As a result, unscrupulous men have got rich, dastardly acts have been committed and communities have been led astray. All because "the Bible says …."

It seems to me that when confusion and uncertainty reign, going back to origins is no bad thing. As Christians, who do we take as the ultimate authority? Jesus, of course. Then surely, in terms of the Scriptures available to him in his day (the Old Testament), we must read them through the eyes of Jesus, a 1st Century Jew. To do this we don't necessarily need a knowledge of Hebrew and Aramaic, the written languages of Scripture in those days. What we do need is to get inside their heads and follow the thought processes that drove their understanding.

The trouble is that the modern Church is not so equipped, nether do many of its number seem interested in the *Jesus mindset*, but seem content to re-interpret the Hebraic mindset through 21st Century Greek structures and culturally "progressive" ideas. There is no real answer to this, looking at the church as a whole, until those in power actively seek to change. All I can do is provide a few signposts, which I have in my trilogy of books, *Hebraic Church, Livin' the Life* and *Shalom* and hope that, when the penny does finally drop, they will have a place to start again (along with many other places, as I grudgingly concede that there are other books by other authors that are helpful too!)

Over the last few years I have heard many a "progressive" liberal Christian exclaim with confident certainty, there's no way Brexit / Trump / Boris are from God! What they should be saying is that these "horrible subversive crazinesses" don't fit in with their view of Who God is and what God does! Fake News may have got caught up in their thinking on a superficial level, but Fake Faith is very much at the centre of their thinking, I believe. This is because, by my way of thinking, which I would like to think is the traditional historical Biblical position, God is not limited by our ideas of what He should be doing. God does what God does and if this includes mandating the European Referendum result and the improbable candidates for Heads of State of Western democracies, then it is up to us to ask, *how do we fit in with all of this*, rather than *how can we stop this madness?*

Liberal Christianity, triggered by Aquinas letting out the Aristotelian genie from the bottle, then fed by generations of rationalists and humanists, has surely chattered itself into irrelevance. *Fake Faith* thrives when Christians let go of the certainties and uncomfortable truths at the heart of our faith. God created the world in six days and then had a little rest. How do I know? The Bible tells me so. Noah and his family were the only ones to survive the worldwide flood. How do I know? The Bible tells me so. The Jews are still a People of promise and have not been rejected by God. How do I know? The Bible tells me so. Yes, these views are not shared by the majority of Christians in our country, but that just shows you how the Bible has been shoved to one side in favour of compromise and expediency. It's an indictment on the Church. Those with *Fake Faith* may still be saved, as long as they haven't jettisoned the key central truths of our faith, but they are never going to be effective in their witness in a post-modern world that feeds on their uncertainties and compromise and sees them as *one of their own*.

The Ninth Commandment may tell us, *you shall not give false testimony against your neighbour,* but could very easily be interpreted (due to the flexibility of Biblical Hebrew) as *you shall not give false testimony* **to** *your neighbour.*

Let us seek to be people of Truth in every way.

God's tenth word – Covet

25

"You shall not covet your neighbor's house. You shall not covet your neighbor's wife, or his male or female servant, his ox or donkey, or anything that belongs to your neighbor." (Exodus 20:17).

This has become ...

There is nothing wrong with having the ambition to strive to legally acquire what you don't have. There is nothing wrong with fulfilling your desires.

As we saw earlier, the World has turned this particular Commandment on its head, actively promoting covetousness as a lifestyle choice and a vital cog in the wheels of capitalism and our consumer society. But what about the Church? Are we any different?

Frankly, in a world where a Bible alone is insufficient to leading a fulfilled Christian life, we must concede that our Christian subculture is just a reflection of the World. Worship has transitioned from being a verb (implying action) to a noun (physical objects). We have a globe-hopping cadre of "worship leaders" with their merchandising, including DVDs, downloads or media streams of their "worship music". We have websites and magazines devoted to this, with reviews and Top Tens and published itineraries. Is this an aspect of covetousness, in the sense of *having to have the latest offering*, or am I being harsh? To be honest, there's a touch of devilish advocacy going on here as I am, in my very small way, part of the "Christian subculture" and hence *part of the problem*.

I write books (*too many*, some may say). Am I promoting covetousness when I promote and advertise them? Does the Christian world actually need them? Could they live without them? I'll leave you to judge. I'd like to think that I have something different to bring to the table, but that could just be self-delusion. Do you all really need the latest Steve Maltz book? I suppose if, by owning one or two of them, rather them coveting what you have, they might actually feel sorry for you! Hah!

Of course, as individual Christians we have a choice whether to partake in this circus, or even just to dip in for an occasional 'splash about'. The ideal situation would be to be in such a close relationship with the Lord that you only purchase resources when He leads you, rather than through an advertising campaign in a Christian magazine, or because your friend has something that *you really must read*.

So a good plan would be one of contentment. Be satisfied with what you have unless the Lord graciously nudges you otherwise. And, of course, keep away from your neighbour's wife, ox, donkey and servant. That goes without saying.

And that's all I am going to say on the subject.

God's final word ?

When Moses came down from the mountain clutching those stone tablets, little did he know that, thousands of years later, the same etched words on stone monuments were going to cause such division and consternation! But God knew, of course, He knew that, in the culture of the western world in the 21st Century, His laws would transition into the *Sinner's Charter*. But the real issue would be with His people, the Church of the western world in the 21st Century. They have simply lost sight of the certainties etched into stone by the Finger of God, bamboozled by their inability to adapt to the shifting sands of the western mindset that moved swiftly from a Christian base, to the rationality of secular humanism, then to the emotional irrationality of the post-modern Marxism that now holds sway. We now live in a culture riddled with relativism, where truths and Truth are always to be doubted and selectively chosen to fit whatever narrative we are comfortable with. Consequently, our set of ten laws are moulded to fit circumstances, as slaves rather than masters.

The job of the Church is to *accept* that they have lost sight of the certainties of God's Laws. If it continues in denial, then it will sink into irrelevance, but if individual Christians wake up to the situation, then there's still a chance before it is too late. The attitude that needs to be expressed is, *if God once gave these laws to mankind then, if He hasn't changed, then surely they haven't changed too?* Instead, the attitude that seems to be followed by most of the

Church is, *Yes, God gave mankind these laws, but surely mankind has changed, so should our interpretation of the laws change?*

Here's a key Bible passage, mentioned earlier, that should drive our thinking:

Do not conform to the pattern of this world, but be transformed by the renewing of your mind. Then you will be able to test and approve what God's will is—his good, pleasing and perfect will. (Romans 12:2).

A much travelled and bookmarked verse, but with great power in its simple truth, the importance of clear, Godly thinking.

Let us remind ourselves of the journey from Sinai to the Senate. We started with certainty:

And God spoke all these words: "I am the LORD your God, who brought you out of Egypt, out of the land of slavery. You shall have no other gods before me. You shall not make for yourself an image in the form of anything in heaven above or on the earth beneath or in the waters below. You shall not bow down to them or worship them; for I, the LORD your God, am a jealous God, punishing the children for the sin of the parents to the third and fourth generation of those who hate me, but showing love to a thousand generations of those who love me and keep my commandments. You shall not misuse the name of the LORD your God, for the LORD will not hold anyone guiltless who misuses his name. Remember the Sabbath day by keeping it holy. Six days you shall labor and do all your work, but the seventh day is a sabbath to the LORD your God. On it you shall not do any work, neither you, nor your son or daughter, nor your male or female servant, nor your animals, nor any foreigner residing in your towns. For in six days the LORD made the heavens

and the earth, the sea, and all that is in them, but he rested on the seventh day. Therefore the LORD blessed the Sabbath day and made it holy. Honour your father and your mother, so that you may live long in the land the LORD your God is giving you. You shall not murder. You shall not commit adultery. You shall not steal. You shall not give false testimony against your neighbor. You shall not covet your neighbor's house. You shall not covet your neighbor's wife, or his male or female servant, his ox or donkey, or anything that belongs to your neighbor." (Exodus 20:1-17).

Although these laws formed the bedrock for national legal systems, they never sustained any kind of prominence in the Church. They have been eclipsed by creeds, dominated by issues of personal salvation, rather than standards of behaviour. The Church has a better track record for saving souls than in training souls. As a result, it has lost sight of the certainties of Laws once given by God to His people. Let's remind ourselves by posing questions:

"You shall have no other gods before me."

Has the Church allowed any leeway to "other gods"? The "gods" of Islam and Hinduism are most definitely "other gods" so any attempt at a *merger* (Chrislam), a compromise (yoga, new age practices) or even *gestures* (Muslim prayers in Cathedrals) are **breaking the First commandment.** Be warned.

"You shall not make for yourself an image in the form of anything in heaven above or on the earth beneath or in the waters below. You shall not bow down to them or worship them ..."

Is our worship 100% directed towards God, our Creator? If even a crumb of adoration falls at the feet of our worship leaders, or our pastors, or any substitute, however worthy it may seem, then we are **breaking the Second commandment.** This is also true if we worship money, success, even our own wife or children. Be warned.

"You shall not misuse the name of the LORD your God, for the LORD will not hold anyone guiltless who misuses his name".

Our culture runs fast and loose with casual blasphemies, where the greater sin is committed if you disrespect a member of a "victim group" rather than Jesus Christ. His very name is brandished as an exclamation, rather than a statement of adoration. What of you and me? Do we regularly audit our speech patterns, even for what may seem innocuous? It may not be for Him, who holds no-one guiltless and so we may very well be **breaking the Third commandment on a regular basis!**

"Remember the Sabbath day by keeping it holy ..."

This is the most neglected of all by the Church, intentionally so. It's been a running sore throughout Church history, fuelled by anti-Semitism and a misunderstanding of Jesus' mindset, interpreting His silence on maintaining the tradition as a directive to cease one of God's Holy Commandments. The move to a Sunday has not helped the situation, as the form has not reflected the function in terms of exactly what God commanded us to do on the 'day of rest'. For this reason, we sadly have to admit that the majority of the Church is **intentionally breaking the Fourth commandment.**

"Honour your father and your mother, so that you may live long in the land the LORD your God is giving you".

The point to make here is that, if we are truly governed by Biblical principles, then we simply can't behave as much of the world does on the issue of caring for aged parents. Great sacrifice may be on the cards, even if "our ministry" is perceived to suffer by putting family first. But if we don't then we could be **knowingly breaking the Fifth commandment,** while the world watches and shrugs its shoulders and remarks, *what's so different about these Christians anyway, they act just like us?*

"You shall not murder."

We must not conform to the pattern of this world (Romans 12:1) and so acting in a godly manner is not always the 'way of peace' as others may see it. Our God has killed off many in His Name, through the Flood, or at Sodom and Gomorrah, for instance. We need His perspective on the sanctity and the taking of human life and although this issue is not going to impact most of us directly, we need to see the distinctions between "unlawful" murder and "lawful" killing. We also need to decide if society is **breaking the Sixth commandment** on issues such as abortion and euthanasia.

"You shall not commit adultery."

Now here's an emotive and difficult subject for the Church, that can't even seem to agree these days on an acceptable definition of what marriage is. But God came up with the concept and has been very clear on this issue and its importance to Him. Perhaps those in leadership need to remind themselves of Jesus's proclamation in Matthew 19:1-12. Also, with the level of Christian divorces running almost as high as in the secular world there needs to be serious consideration of the implications and circumstances and whether there is an issue with **breaking the Seventh commandment?** One thing to remember is that we are not called to judge and point fingers, as there could very well be extenuating circumstances, but God is always the ultimate judge.

"You shall not steal."

This is not as trivial a matter as it is often made out to be. We Christians must examine ourselves and our motives and always consider that the gift of life is a gift from God, as is the gift of time allotted to us and the gift of finances that He allows to pass through our hands. Are we making the best use of these gifts because, if we are not returning the favour to Him through the way we interact with the world and His Church, then we could very well be **breaking the Eighth commandment?**

"You shall not give false testimony against your neighbour."

In a culture that positively revels in untruths and gossip, we Christians are in real danger of being sucked into this madness. We need to be people of the Truth, not just in the everyday business of avoiding lies (even white lies and minor peccadillos) but in the Eternal Truths passed to us through Scripture and revelation. Is our version of the Truth the right one? Are we reading the Bible correctly? These things need to concern us, otherwise we are not being the best witnesses for our God and could be unconsciously **breaking the Ninth commandment** in principle, through giving a false witness, as we see with the "Jehovah's Witnesses".

"You shall not covet your neighbour's house. You shall not covet your neighbour's wife, or his male or female servant, his ox or donkey, or anything that belongs to your neighbour."

Our capitalist world feeds on covetousness, it's what

makes it work. Are we being sucked in, also? So we need to examine ourselves and consider whether we have joined the world in **breaking the Tenth commandment.**

So a bit of honesty is probably in order. Also, to remind ourselves that Jesus himself kept the Ten Commandments and promoted them too:

We know that we have come to know him if we keep his commands. Whoever says, "I know him," but does not do what he commands is a liar, and the truth is not in that person. But if anyone obeys his word, love for God is truly made complete in them. This is how we know we are in him: Whoever claims to live in him must live as Jesus did. (1 John 2:3-6).

So don't let anyone deflect you with the old *that's Old Testament stuff, we've moved on from there!* The Ten Commandments applied to Jesus in his earthly life and they apply to us now too. The only difference between us and Old Testament Jews is that we have the law written on our hearts (Jeremiah 31:31-35) and our hearts have been renewed by grace. This plain fact has sadly been overlooked or ignored by many in the Church, that law and grace are not at odds with each other, but, instead *must work together.*

For the grace of God has appeared that offers salvation to all people. It teaches us to say "No" to ungodliness and worldly passions, and to live self-controlled, upright and godly lives in this present age (Titus 2:11-12).

The rest is up to us. We need to reclaim these Ten Commandments as relevant to our generation, even to a Church that seems to trivialise the need for conduct based on given Laws. We need to keep them and then teach them to others. Then, perhaps, the World will sit up and notice us a people of hope and certainty.

Now why don't you ... ?

At the current time twenty four of Steve's books are available for purchase, either through Christian bookshops or directly from *www.sppublishing.com*

Shalom : *God's Masterplan*

Is today's Church what God originally intended it to be? How can One New Man be achieved and how it can bring renewal to the Church.

Into the Lion's Den : *Reaching a world gone mad*

Daniel was tested in the lions' den. Today, Christians must venture into a very different lion's den and wake up to what is probably the greatest current threat to our witness to the World.

Noise : *A search for sense*

Noise is everywhere, invading all of our five senses. This incisive, surprising and entertaining book cuts through to the heart of the issue. Is there meaning in the mayhem that has become our World?

To Life! *Rediscovering Biblical Church*

Have you ever asked the question, where does the World end and the Church begin? Is the 21st Century Church truly the best it could possibly be?

How the Church lost The Way...
... and how it can find it again

The story of how the Church has been infiltrated by a pagan virus that has worked its way through every facet of our Christian life and how we can start fighting back.

How the Church lost The Truth...
... and how it can find it again

What has happened to some key battlegrounds of Christian Truth and how it is that the Church has managed to lose so much that had been revealed to it in the Bible.

Jesus, the Man of Many Names :
A Fresh Understanding from the dawn of time to the End of Days

A book about Jesus that does offer fresh insights without boasting new revelations. Drawing on sources from the Jewish world, ancient and modern, the author will take you on an exhilarating, lively and entertaining exploration of the life and times of the Jewish Messiah.

The Truth is out there :
The Ultimate World Conspiracy. Who really is pulling the strings?

Is history just a random sequence of events, or are there secret manipulations? What makes us tick? How did the World as we see it come to be? Read this book if you are prepared to be challenged.

The (other) F-Word : Faith, the Last Taboo

A presentation of the Gospel for the modern world. It is direct, uncompromising, engaging and is written to be relevant to the everyday person. Dare you go where modern man fears to tread? You'll either be inspired or provoked, either way it should be an interesting experience.

Outcast Nation : *Israel, The Jews ... and You*

The story of the People and the Land through biblical and secular history, tracing the outworkings of God's covenants and offering explanations for both the survival and the success of this Outcast Nation.

God's Signature :
The Wonders of the Hebrew Scriptures

Have you ever wondered how the Old Testament came to be written, why God chose Hebrew as the language of the Book and what exactly could we be missing through not reading the Hebrew Scriptures in their original language?

The Bishop's New Clothes :
Has the Church Sold out to the World?

Is the Church as it should be or has it sold out to the World? Is the Body of Christ doing all it could as God's ambassadors or is there room for not so much an improvement as a complete overhaul? This book pulls no punches, but it does so engagingly, with wit and warmth.

God's Blueprint :
What does the Old Testament really say?

You will discover recurring themes that build up a wonderful picture of God, the actions and teachings of the Biblical prophets in context, the benefits of viewing the Scriptures Hebraically and new insights revealed by the One New Man Bible translation.

God's Tapestry :
What do we do with the Hebrew Scriptures?

This book scratches where most of the Church is itching and cuts right to the heart of some of the controversies concerning how we should be reading and acting on God's Word today.

Hebraic Church : *Thinking Differently*

Hebraic Church? Now there's a phrase designed to upset or confuse just about everyone. Yet being Hebraic is not what many in the Church imagines it to be. In fact it could be nothing less than the key for true restoration and revival. Hope Is there any hope in the World? Here is a book written to stir the heart of the average citizen of today's world by challenging them to think beyond the here and now. It pulls no punches as it provides a creeping crescendo of revelation regarding man and his relationship with God and how the Church has mostly failed in its mission to mirror the image of Jesus.

Livin' the Life : *Christianity rediscovered*

Using tools developed over the last few years, the author re-examines a wide spectrum of what we think and how we act as followers of Jesus Christ. To move forwards in our faith we really need to go back to the very beginning.

Hope

Here is a book written to stir the heart of the average citizen of today's world by challenging them to think beyond the here and now. It pulls no punches as it provides a creeping crescendo of revelation regarding man and his relationship with God and how the Church has mostly failed in its mission to mirror the image of Jesus.

Zionion : *Why does the World obsess over Israel?*

What's with the British government, the Palestinians, the United Nations, the media, activists, academics, boycotters, some Jews (!), Jihadists, some Christians, neo-Nazis and conspiracy buffs?

The Christmas Telling : *The Nativity around your table*

It is time to rescue Christmas from the encroaching trappings of our materialistic culture. Wouldn't it be nice to experience the full Nativity story in a safe place, with friends and family and using all five senses? Now you can do so in this unique interactive presentation ... and there are real blessings to be had.

The Easter Telling :
Easter explained in a Passover service

In this small booklet you have all that you need to recreate this service, primarily following the script indicated in the Gospel accounts, but always in the context of the events of the Exodus, the backdrop of the Passover celebration.

Water : *The Stuff of Life*

This small book takes you on a fascinating journey into the world of water. From a brief analysis of its structure and unique properties, we look at its function in our bodies and then wonder how it gets to us, through natural means and human ingenuity. We also see its significance in world religions but also see its darker side.

Blood : *The River of Life*

When it comes to connections, nothing does it better than blood. Silently and unseen it performs its tasks within our body. But it doesn't stop there, blood is identified with other functions that stretch into community, heritage and even further into very surprising places.

Bread : *The Food of Life*

This small book explores the world of bread. From its origins and history, we look at how it has been made and see it as a metaphor of how our world has gained a degree of complexity, yet has failed in feeding everyone.